PRAISE FOR *THE MIND ST*

'In these anxious, uncertain times, we
minds cope and even thrive. Dr Jodi
exercises for minds to gain strength and
to face his/her anxiety. Beneficial to both adults and children, .
recommending this book to my friends as a journal of empowerment.
Well done and thank you Dr Lowinger.' **Anthony Field (Blue Wiggle)**

'Jodie has an extraordinary desire to help those struggling with anxiety.
Her knowledge on the topic of anxiety is quite remarkable, so too her
drive to make a difference to peoples' lives. *The Mind Strength Method*
is hugely beneficial to anyone looking to get the best out of both themselves and those around them. At a time when the world is struggling
with anxiety and depression, programs such as Jodie's truly make a
difference.' **Hugh Van Cuylenberg, author of *The Resilience Project***

'This book is a practical and useful resource for working through anxiety.
Dr Jodie approaches anxiety in a beautiful way, and her method has
helped me so much … I know it will help many others work through
anxiety. I can't wait to share it with the world!' **Laura Henshaw, Co-
Founder of Keep It Cleaner and author of *A Girl's Guide to Kicking Goals***

'*The Mind Strength Method* is a "must read" for anyone suffering
anxiety or dealing with stress. Simple and achievable tools for navigating
a busy and unpredictable lifestyle, which is most of us really! Combining
the fundamentals of neuroscience, psychology and positive thinking,
The Mind Strength Method is the "Google maps" for navigating
anxiety, stress and a busy life. Outstanding.' **Associate Professor Ralph
Mobbs, one of Sydney's leading neurosurgeons and neuroscientists**

'Kiss your old life and habits goodbye! Dr Jodie delivers multiple
lightbulb moments as she shows readers the true strength we each
possess for real mental change – both personally and professionally.'
Robin Roberson, Managing Director of Claim Central North America

'Dr Jodie combines outstanding skills as a high-performance coach to
global executives and organisations and an anxiety and mindset expert.
Her book, *The Mind Strength Method*, will help both individuals and
organisations succeed and is a must-read to help you through these
challenging times.' **Thomas Vikstrom, Founding Senior Engineer, Tesla,
and Co-founder, TNTX**

'Dr Jodie's *The Mind Strength Method* is a must! Her calm and constant nature is unique, as is her empathetic and encouraging take on building resilience and courage, and overcoming adversity. Her advice and techniques help tackle challenging situations in a constructive and uncomplicated manner. This mood-boosting book is packed with positive and practical ways to live the best life you can, create confidence, reduce stress, and take back control of your life.' **Kerrie McCallum, Editor-in-Chief of delicious. and Editorial Director of Sunday Style (*Sunday Telegraph* and *Sunday Herald Sun*)**

'Dr Jodie's step-by-step process to build resilience, optimise performance, and encourage a values-focused outlook comes at just the right moment. As the world grapples with the effects of the pandemic, more and more people will need anti-anxiety toolkits, and Dr Jodie's book can help anyone create their own ... Through filling out worksheets, ticking boxes, and creating actionable plans, every reader will be able to better understand the causes of anxiety and manage their responses to it. Everyone will find something useful in a book like this ... If you or your child wants to build resilience in the face of stress and anxiety, read this book. Now.' **April Palmerlee, CEO of the American Chamber of Commerce in Australia**

'Dr. Jodie Lowinger is absolutely passionate about helping us to manage our anxiety. Her intelligent, practical and positive approach to teaching the skills we all need at certain times of our lives to counter anxious tendencies is effective and invaluable. This is enhanced by her warmth, empathy and determination to make a difference. At this challenging time in society today Jodie Lowinger's book is a must read.' **Lynne Malcolm, Producer of *All in the Mind*, ABC Radio National**

'Jodie has personally helped friends of mine of all ages with their anxiety. She's the perfect person for this year and the tough years ahead.' **Gus Worland, Triple M, CEO Gotcha4Life**

'Dr Jodie is one of our most inspiring speakers and authors. Every single audience has loved her for her great insights, her empathy, her hands on tips and always inspiring words. With great passion, Jodie and her Mind Strength Method are helping corporate audiences around the world to build resilience and high performance and deal with anxiety and uncertainty and we are grateful for the consistent value that she brings.' **Micha Schipper, CEO of Lecture, The Netherlands**

'We live in a fretful age. Certainties are collapsing. Demands are multiplying. Anxiety is an epidemic. Luckily, Dr Lowinger has the measure of your amygdala. In this book she explains the "flight, fight or freeze" response that drives so much of our stress. But her real gift is her techniques for reframing those responses to return power and strength to our daily lives. Read it.' **Hugh Riminton, Journalist**

'Dr Jodie Lowinger's ability to distil down and simplify life's complexities into useful tools that can be applied every day in both personal and professional situations is incredible. I would highly recommend this in both a personal and professional context. Very empowering!' **Brian Siemsen, Global CEO of Claim Central Consolidated, and ex-NRL football player**

'Whether you need help in your personal life, business or both, Jodie's methods are remarkable. I highly recommend her.' **Vince Frost, Founder, CEO and Group Executive Creative Director of Frost* collective**

'An hour with Dr Jodie Lowinger is an hour you will never regret so to be able to access her incredible Mind Strength Method in her new book is fantastic. Now more than ever people of all ages and backgrounds need to learn how to build resilience, reduce and manage stress and find ways to deal with the many challenges that life keeps gifting us. Dr Jodie is the perfect balance of empathy, passion and incredible knowledge and her program is a tool that I firmly believe everyone can benefit from.' **Natalie Moore, Senior Executive, Lendlease**

'Anxiety is rampant in society and in these uncertain times there has never been a better time to have Dr Jodie's *The Mind Strength Method* at hand. Dr Jodie is a wealth of knowledge and her passion to help people live their best life is infectious. We certainly need more people like her out there.' **Dr Lewis Ehrlich, Dentist to the FFA, Former Pro Soccer Player**

'In a world that's changing so fast it's easy to lose your bearings, Jodie's approach provides a steadying compass to see you through modern life's ups and downs. She combines deep empathy with no-nonsense practicality, through a process that's life-affirming, refreshing, and that's been a revelation for us and our children. For insight, for building resilience, and for tools to change your life for the better, we can't recommend her approach highly enough.' **David Peers, Director and Cinematographer (*Happy Feet, Mad Max* amongst others), Co-Founder of Big Serious Studios and Katrina Peers, Co-Founder of Big Serious Studios**

This book is dedicated to my most magnificent treasures, my family. Thank you for being the abundant source for my gratitude. May you live each day with mind strength. Stand up to fear and be guided by your values. From my heart to yours with eternal love.

THE
MIND
STRENGTH
METHOD

Published in 2021 by Murdoch Books,
an imprint of Allen & Unwin

Murdoch Books Australia
83 Alexander Street,
Crows Nest NSW 2065
Phone: +61 (0)2 8425 0100
murdochbooks.com.au
info@murdochbooks.com.au

Murdoch Books UK
Ormond House, 26–27 Boswell Street,
London WC1N 3JZ
Phone: +44 (0) 20 8785 5995
murdochbooks.co.uk
info@murdochbooks.co.uk

 A catalogue record for this
book is available from the
National Library of Australia

A catalogue record for this book is available from the British Library

ISBN 9 781 92235 138 8 Australia
ISBN 9 781 91166 818 3 UK

Cover design by Trisha Garner
Cover image by iStockphoto
Illustrations by Astred Hicks, Design Cherry
Text design, typesetting and infographics by Susanne Geppert
Printed and bound in Australia by Griffin Press

10 9 8 7 6 5 4 3 2 1

The paper in this book is FSC certified.
FSC promotes environmentally responsible,
socially beneficial and economically viable
management of the world's forests.

THE
MIND STRENGTH METHOD

Four steps to curb anxiety, conquer worry & build resilience

DR JODIE LOWINGER

murdoch books

Sydney | London

Contents

Introduction

Chapter 1

Anxiety can be a superpower

If anxiety, stress or worry are preventing you from living a confident, fulfilled life, you're most definitely not alone. Anxiety and stress levels within our society are now at epidemic proportions. In fact, anxiety disorders are the most prevalent of the mental health concerns, with approximately one in four Australian adults, children and adolescents experiencing anxiety at clinical levels in their lifetime – that's anxiety so extreme that it prevents them from living life the way they want to live it. You may not be surprised that research shows these numbers are on the rise.

Anxiety itself is very much a part of our common human experience. It's the result of living in this uncertain, ever-changing world – a result of being human! Our brains are hard-wired to experience anxiety. It is an inherent, self-protective mechanism. If we perceive something to be dangerous or threatening, our brain triggers a stress reaction called the fight or flight response – a neurochemical process that prepares our body to run away or stay and fight to protect ourself against the perceived threat. This is what we experience as anxiety.

However, for some people, anxiety tips into clinical levels. This is where anxiety can wreak havoc on our lives and contribute to tremendous suffering. The good news is that whether you experience day-to-day anxiety or clinical anxiety, the Mind Strength Method will help you.

As a doctor of clinical psychology, an international speaker on anxiety, mindset and resilience, an executive coach and founder of The Anxiety Clinic, I have had the privilege of helping thousands of adults, children and adolescents to find freedom from anxiety and learn to embrace life with confidence, happiness and a true sense of wellbeing.

Through my close work with people who experience anxiety, I can say first-hand that anxiety is not a flaw or a weakness (which is why I avoid words such as 'disorder' or 'illness'). We need to let go of ideas about anxiety meaning you are 'not good enough', which typically lead to feelings of shame. In fact, anxiety can be a superpower. This is because, in my experience, the large majority of people who struggle with anxiety have a beautiful depth of thinking and a rare depth of feeling – a strong, analytical mind combined with an empathic heart. As I like to say, 'You care because you care.'

In my role as an anxiety expert and high-performance coach, I help people to recognise and acknowledge the strengths that often go hand in hand with anxiety. Rather than suffering in silence and stifling these attributes, my clients learn effective ways they can harness and leverage these strengths. They also learn to feel empowered to stand up to their worry and fears, and to tip their mindset and actions towards their values, passion and purpose.

Informed by my years of clinical and corporate research and practice, I have developed the Mind Strength Method, a four-step process to help people of all ages to curb anxiety, conquer worry and build a resilient mindset. The chapters ahead are filled with tools and techniques formulated through my experience helping adults, children and adolescents living with anxiety and stress. These strategies have demonstrated effectiveness to help people overcome fear and turn their lives around.

Combining fundamentals from neuroscience, clinical psychology and positive psychology, the Mind Strength Method is a fourth wave of therapy, built from the best of proven therapeutic approaches, including cognitive behavioural therapy, acceptance and commitment therapy and narrative therapy. My clients have found that the techniques of the Mind Strength Method have helped them with a level of effectiveness they had not previously experienced. Many people, having spent a lot of time and money on various therapies without significant outcome, have been amazed at the transformation they have achieved within a few months using the Mind Strength Method.

That's not to say that I don't believe in medication – I'm a 'hybrid' therapist and recognise that people who experience more severe anxiety may require medication alongside the techniques I teach. The choice to prescribe medication is always made following a discussion with a client's doctor, who is able to prescribe the most suitable treatment for them. But regardless of whether or not medication has been prescribed, the Mind Strength Method can help you.

So would you (or your child, partner or friend) like to find freedom from worry, anxiety, fear and stress? Would you like to learn to engage in life with confidence, positivity and success? If the answer is yes, then this book is most definitely for you. I look forward to sharing my life's work to help you live your life with renewed courage, resilience, happiness and wellbeing.

Dr Jodie

Chapter 2

A story of courage

You can't always change the situation –
but you can change how you respond to it

At the very heart of the Mind Strength Method is courage – the courage to stand up to fear and to be guided instead by a path aligned with your values. This forms the roadmap to overcoming anxiety and living a fulfilled life.

The key to this is building resilience. Resilience is not about bad things not happening – adversity is, after all, a normal part of being human. Resilience is our ability to bounce back from challenges. Resilience is about creating the space to choose how you respond to these challenges. Through the Mind Strength Method, we learn to recognise that the situation is not always in our control but we have the capacity to choose how we respond to it. As the brilliant psychiatrist Viktor Frankl writes in *Man's Search for Meaning*, 'Between stimulus and response there is a space. In that space is our power to choose our response. In our response lies our growth and our freedom.'

My own family's story is remarkably similar to Viktor Frankl's. His memoir describes life in the Nazi death camp

Auschwitz during World War II. Based on his own experiences and the stories of death and survival around him, Frankl states that strength doesn't lie in avoidance of suffering but rather in our capacity to make purposeful choices in how we respond to adversity. It lies in our ability to stand up to adversity and to realign with what gives us a sense of meaning. In fact, Frankl writes, our primary drive is not towards pleasure but, rather, towards meaning. It is an inherent human drive that offers us a way to move beyond suffering, and find renewed energy, hope and resilience by realigning to our purpose and values.

In fact, this power to respond to adversity with resilience has enabled me to be here, writing this book and sharing my expertise to help others. The essence of the Mind Strength Method is core to my family's story of survival – a family history that has motivated me to encourage people around the globe to be empowered to stand up to fear and to seek a life of meaning, purpose and fulfilment.

My family's story is also one of strength and courage achieved through engagement with meaning. It begins with Elsa, a sweet-natured 19-year-old girl from Topolcany, a small town in Slovakia in the heart of Europe. Elsa had two older sisters, Mancika and Zlata. Zlata had a beautiful baby girl named Veronika, whom Elsa adored.

One day the soldiers came. Elsa was separated from her family and taken on a cattle train to Auschwitz. Alone and terrified, Elsa was ordered into the line of people who were given jobs. The others were sent to the gas chambers to die.

Elsa's job was to sort through the belongings of all the people who were brought to Auschwitz. It was there that a

miracle occurred. Elsa came across this photo. This is a photo of Veronika; this is a photo of my mother.

Elsa picked up the photo and hid it in her sparse clothes at the risk of being discovered and killed. That evening she concealed it in a crack between the bricks near her bunk bed. She looked at this photo every night. It was this photo that helped Elsa to hold onto her values, her purpose, what was important to her; it was this photo that enabled her to stand up to fear and gave her the strength and courage to survive.

So what had happened to little Veronika? Soon after Elsa was taken to Auschwitz, Veronika was taken with her parents, Zlata and Joseph, her grandmother 'Omama', and her aunt Mancika to a labour camp (the precursor to the death camp). There she lived under soldier guard for two years. When

Veronika was three, the Slovak National Uprising occurred. In the labour camp, soldiers began shooting and Veronika was separated from her parents; she had to flee into a forest with her aunt and grandmother to escape death. They came to a farm and it was there that they were hidden in a barn by strangers – people who stood up to the fear of losing their own lives by aligning with a value of helping others. Unable to remain in the barn for long, Veronika, her aunt and her grandmother walked on, continuing their journey towards survival with a determination fuelled by love. Then another miracle occurred. They were taken in by a woman who hid them in an attic alongside 14 other strangers. There they remained for more than six months, until the end of World War II and liberation.

This is my family's story. That, at the tender age of three, my mother was separated from her parents under terrifying circumstances. That her father, my grandfather Joseph, hid for six months in a self-made underground bunker in the forest, holding on to the hope of seeing his loved ones again. And her mother, my grandmother Zlata, also empowered by love and the hope of being reunited with family, was able to obtain false papers and find work as a nanny for a doctor's child, who also risked her life for the value of helping others. And that her aunt, Elsa, was finally reunited into the arms of her family in Topolcany months after the end of the war.

This is the core of my foundations. It is a story of courage, strength, and resilience, built on alignment with purpose, meaning and values. It is about the human capacity to stand up to fear and choose how we respond in any given set of circumstances. However, when a person is born into displacement, murder and separation from her parents, an anxious tempera-ment evolves. My mother, Veronika, was born into such terror and so I was born into anxiety. I was born as a parent to my mother – a caregiver from the very beginning.

There began my passion for helping others to overcome anxiety. It has been a yearning, a calling, from a young age. At high school, my passion for psychology was demonstrated in my major artwork, which was a series of paintings on emotions in children. I became determined to work out how to help people to conquer anxiety and build resilience. At university, I researched the early contributors to anxiety, with a view to building anxiety prevention programs in schools. In 2014, I set up the Sydney Anxiety Clinic (now The Anxiety Clinic), offering evidence-based therapy for anxiety, stress, mood, behavioural challenges and traumatic life experiences for adults, children and adolescents. Alongside this, I established mind strength peak performance, resilience and wellbeing programs to help leaders and teams in organisations, and educators and students in schools, to build the mindset and skills to succeed. My work has culminated in the development of the Mind Strength Method, which has helped thousands of people – in both a personal *and* professional context – of all ages to conquer worry, manage anxiety, boost mood and build resilience. And it is this method that I have the pleasure of sharing with you here.

Chapter 3

Welcome to the Mind Strength Method

*Practical, simple and effective
strategies to turn your life around*

There is no doubt that anxiety, low mood and stress can have an overwhelming negative impact, preventing us from leading the life we want to live. The Mind Strength Method has been proven to help individuals overcome anxiety and effectively turn their lives around. In the chapters ahead, I will guide you through each stage of the Mind Strength Method and the simple strategies you can implement to work towards a life of satisfaction, resilience, wellbeing and success. Specifically, these tools and techniques will help you and your loved ones to

- conquer worry, fear, anxiety and stress
- boost mood
- resolve sleep difficulties
- overcome imposter syndrome
- build emotional resilience

- take steps out of your comfort zone
- better manage bullies or challenging relationships at work or school
- improve relationships
- face and conquer phobias
- move to a less fearful and more positive outlook on life
- boost confidence, assertiveness and self-belief
- reduce health anxiety
- stop avoidance behaviours and feel happy and calm
- bolster yourselves against burnout
- embrace change and uncertainty
- build grit and a growth mindset
- gain clarity on values and purpose
- optimise productivity, performance and success.

The Mind Strength Method will first help you to demystify anxiety. Together we will go through the neuroscience of anxiety – which is, in essence, a physiological reaction to worry thoughts, or the fight or flight reaction. You will learn to conceptualise worry as a bully that bosses you around. I will equip you with a Mind Strength Toolkit to boss worry back, gradually approach avoided situations and let go of unhelpful coping strategies. You will reflect on which values are important to you and learn to develop the mind strength to find freedom from anxiety and build a mindset for happiness and fulfilment – a life aligned with what's most important to YOU, not with what worry is telling you.

Let's start by exploring the four stages of the Mind Strength Method.

STEP 1 – Awareness of your fight or flight driven thoughts, feelings and actions

You can only change what you
are aware of in the first place

The Mind Strength Method begins with building self-awareness. Core to self-awareness is creating the space to reflect on whether your thoughts, feelings and actions are driven by fear, anger or low mood, or whether they are driven by your purpose and values. This is a concrete way to differentiate between thoughts that are unhelpful or helpful in any given moment.

In Step 1, we explore

* the situations that trigger the fight or flight reaction
* how you feel in those situations
* what you do in those situations.

Your fight or flight driven reactions – what you do when you perceive a threat in your environment – serve a fundamental purpose in protecting you in times of *real* threat. If you are being attacked, your most logical course of action (perhaps your only course of action) may well be to fight, to hide or to run. In these moments, your body's ability to engage your fight or flight response is an incredibly powerful and critical self-protective mechanism.

However, in times of *perceived* threat – when you are just worried about the future or ruminating about the past – the emotional, behavioural and physiological experiences of the fight or flight response typically prove counterproductive and unhelpful. These situations of perceived threat can tip you into anger, agitation, despair, anxiety and stress, when you actually want to be able to engage with self-awareness. This book will give you the capacity to move out of fight or flight, quieten your hijacking amygdala (more of which later) and the anxiety or anger response, and realign with a more helpful pathway – one that is aligned with your purpose, values, emotionally intelligent engagement (see page 53) and resilience. The Mind Strength Method will help you to regain this control.

STEP 2 – Awareness of your values

Reflect on what gives you a sense of meaning and fulfilment

The next step is gaining self-awareness of your values. Values are those elements in your life that give you a sense of meaning, happiness and fulfilment. Values-driven actions are those behaviours aligned with the direction you want to go in life (as opposed to the direction in which fear, anger, anxiety or depression are taking you). Values-driven actions are helpful actions that will give you your greatest chance of a life of satisfaction, wellbeing and success. In this step, I encourage you to start to reflect on the things that are important to you and to consider some of the things that you would love to do but fear gets in the way. This is an insight into the path ahead.

STEP 3 – The Mind Strength Toolkit

Powerful, effective strategies to build resilience

In order to have the power to stand up to the fight or flight reaction and realign with your values and purpose, you need to build resilience. In this step, I share my Mind Strength Toolkit, which gives you proven strategies to boost your emotional intelligence, mental strength and wellbeing. These tools will help you to feel empowered and develop the skills and strategies required to achieve mind strength.

STEP 4 – Move forward aligned with your values and purpose

What we focus on grows

The final step is being able to move forward in life aligned with your values and purpose. Clarity on your values is powerful; however, clarity alone is not enough. Step 4 involves establishing a plan to engage in purposeful action. This values-driven plan combines

- your values and purpose
- values-driven goals
- goal-driven actions
- a wellbeing action plan.

Being equipped with a clear, alternative pathway makes it a little easier to stand up to the voice of worry and alleviate the anxiety that can so readily hijack the brain in any given moment. Building a wellbeing action plan will bolster your resilience and sustainability over the long term.

While our circumstances are not always in our control, we have the power to create the space to choose how we respond to the situation. In the case of perceived threat, we want to stand up to an anger-driven pathway (fight) or fear-driven pathway (flight) and instead engage in resilience and wellbeing strategies that align with our purpose and values.

———

Now that I've introduced you to the four steps of the Mind Strength Method, let's meet some of my clients who have used this method to help conquer their anxiety, build resilience and lead a more satisfying and successful life.

THE MIND STRENGTH METHOD

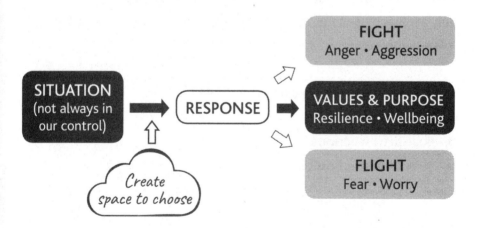

Chapter 4

Meet the case studies

In my work at The Anxiety Clinic, and as a high-performance and executive coach, I have helped people just like you and of all ages who are working hard to manage anxiety and build a life of satisfaction and wellbeing. Throughout this book, we will follow the lives of some of these individuals more closely and see how the Mind Strength Method has worked for them. Have a think about whether you can relate to any of the challenges these individuals have experienced. The content of our worries and life situation might be a little different from person to person but our brains and emotions respond in fairly consistent ways. There is power and hopefulness in this – because if the strategies have helped others, they can help you too, quickly, effectively and permanently.

MEET MIKE I worked with Mike, a 48-year-old father of three and business executive, as his high-performance coach. When we commenced our work together, he was in a dark place, experiencing severe anxiety, high agitation, stress and low mood. Mike's specific goals were to reduce his stress and anxiety, boost his mood, improve his overall performance, and enhance his sense of wellbeing.

Mike and his wife had both worked hard throughout their lives, but with the increasing cost of living, Mike worried that he wouldn't have enough money to fund all they needed for the future. His wife reassured him that they would be fine, but he still felt anxious and believed he needed to work harder in order to ensure that they were financially secure. He also had begun worrying about his health as the years progressed. He checked the internet to make sure that his symptoms didn't mean that something terrible was happening. He had started getting more regular check-ups with his family doctor and specialists, just in case.

Mike found that he was becoming increasingly agitated as time went on. He had a short fuse more frequently and his anger was escalating. He was lashing out verbally from time to time, both at home and at work, and he had shouted at his wife and kids on several occasions. This was a side of himself that he didn't like: he considered himself to be quite a calm and positive person, and this behaviour distressed him and his family. Mike began having a few drinks in the evening to try to calm his stress levels. His emotions were starting to get the better of him and he found himself feeling increasingly despondent and down. He even had some dark thoughts from time to time about how he could escape when things were becoming too tough.

Case Study

MEET ELLA When I met Ella, a 36-year-old mother of two and corporate professional, she was experiencing high levels of distress. Worry was overwhelming her, particularly at night. She worried that she was going to let her family down and feared that she was going to make mistakes at work. She wished that she could feel more confident and assertive, particularly in work situations. She repeatedly second-guessed herself and despite her continued professional progress, she felt as though she didn't deserve her success. She didn't feel like she truly knew what she was doing and was concerned that people would discover that she actually wasn't any good.

Ella also worried that something bad was going to happen to her children. She wanted to make sure that she was giving her best as a mum. She repeatedly checked on her kids and felt guilty that she had to spend time at work and away from them. Ella took a lot of pride in the family home and worked hard to ensure that the home environment was 'perfect'. She also felt that she was forever looking after everyone and everything and that nobody appreciated the work she was doing. She rarely had any down time and was stressed about the constant chores she felt she had to do. She had a loving relationship with her husband, but she worried that he didn't understand the extent of her workload.

Ella's stress levels were through the roof and she couldn't find windows in her day to get to the gym or to do the things that she liked. She was feeling frazzled and experiencing disturbed sleep at night. As a result, her mood was deteriorating, and she was beginning to withdraw from activities that she used to enjoy, such as catching up with friends. She was exhausted and overwhelmed. Life was becoming increasingly hard.

Case Study

MEET ALLIE Allie, a 22-year-old student working part-time in a cafe, came to see me at The Anxiety Clinic with increasing self-doubt and stress. She told me she had experienced some tricky times in school with other girls who had been mean to her. Now at university, she found that she was getting more and more frazzled in tutorials and did not want to speak up in case she said something incorrect or embarrassing. She knew the answers to questions, but had lots of self-doubt about whether what she wanted to say would be correct.

Allie had some good friends but she second-guessed herself in social situations. She was becoming increasingly anxious at parties and felt a bit stressed out before going out with her friends. It was particularly bad when she was getting ready for a date, and sometimes she decided not to go at all because she was concerned that something bad might happen. She worried that she was not attractive and thought that she was overweight. She compared herself to her friends and believed that they were prettier and more popular. She also checked her phone frequently to make sure that her friends weren't doing things without her, and spent a long time making sure that her own posts were perfect.

Allie worried that she wouldn't be able to find a good enough job and feared that the cost of living was skyrocketing with day-to-day expenses. She wanted to spend money on doing things to look and feel good enough but was increasingly stressed out that she wasn't able to afford it. She was concerned about the environment and the events happening in the world that would make her future unsafe. She felt quite helpless.

Case Study

MEET ADAM When I met Adam, a 16-year-old high school student, he was experiencing high stress and anxiety over exams and assignments. He worried about failing his exams and found it hard to focus when doing his homework or trying to study. It was difficult for him to get to sleep at night because he was focusing on all the things that might go wrong. The more he worried, the more anxious he felt and the more he feared that he wouldn't be good enough.

He procrastinated even though he wanted to do well, and spent hours on social media and playing computer games rather than doing his work because it helped reduce his stress. Adam knew what he needed to do and how to do it – but he just couldn't help it. He felt that being on the internet was a helpful escape for him; he met people there he could connect with, and he found himself turning to this more and more. It began to get in the way of him going out and getting on with things. He started going to sleep later and later, which meant that he was exhausted the next day, which in turn made it hard to focus on his work and activities. His performance started to suffer, which then increased his stress levels, and a difficult spiral started to take hold.

Adam was agitated at home, resulting in a lot of conflict between him and his parents. His mum and dad were at a loss as to what they could do to help. They couldn't understand what had gone wrong, when it used to be so easy. They needed some practical strategies to help Adam get through high school successfully and live a happier life.

MEET LUKE Eleven-year-old Luke came to The Anxiety Clinic with his parents, seeking help to overcome his fear of dogs. He had never had a particularly bad experience with dogs; his fear had just escalated over time. Luke and his parents reported that he avoided any situations where there was a chance a dog would be there, such as going to the park or the beach. He would cross the road if he saw a dog walking up ahead, even if it happened to be on a leash. He avoided going to his friends' houses if they had a dog, and his parents would agree to invite them to his house instead.

Over time Luke's fear had increased to the point that he avoided reading books if he knew a dog was in the story. His fear and avoidance were getting so extreme that he even felt anxious if somebody used the word 'dog', and he had started to think twice about leaving the house. Luke would sometimes feel like he had to carry a water bottle or stick, which he could use to fend off a dog should he ever be attacked. His parents reported that he tended to pick up on stories in the news about bad things that had happened with dogs, which kept him trapped in his fear. He felt safe as long as he didn't come into contact with a dog. He sometimes came into his parents' room at night due to bad dreams, and would check with them about upcoming parties and sporting events to make sure that they weren't located in parks where dogs were allowed off leash or where families had dogs. Luke's fears were starting to take over the day-to-day running of the household, and his parents were at a loss as to what they should do.

● ● ●

Perhaps there are a few things in Mike, Ella, Allie, Adam and Luke's lives that are familiar to you or to your family? While the content and experiences of worry, anxiety and stress are different across individuals, the processes play out in similar ways. This means that no matter whether the anxiety, worry, low mood or stress we experience is mild, moderate or severe, we can identify and adopt consistent strategies that have a powerful and positive impact for everyone.

The good news is that Mike, Ella, Allie, Adam, Luke and their loved ones were all able to learn highly effective ways to build mind strength – and you can, too!

––––––

In the chapters to come, we will work through the four steps of the Mind Strength Method, and you will learn how to live the life that you choose to live, not the life that worry is dictating to you. I look forward to keeping you company throughout the pages ahead. Let's do this!

STEP

1

Awareness of your fight or flight driven thoughts, feelings and actions

Chapter 5

What is anxiety?

*Anxiety is your physiological reaction
to a perceived threat*

With anxiety at epidemic proportions in our society, there's a critical need to enable people to shift from worry, stress and fear to a happier and more fulfilled life. And, as you now know, it is my heart-driven mission, forged by my own family's story of adversity and courage, to help people to feel empowered to alleviate their anxiety and build mind strength. But when we talk about anxiety, what exactly do we mean?

Anxiety is an essential survival mechanism. It has been with us since primitive times, when life was simple and things in our surroundings were either friend or foe. What mattered most back then, in much the same way as it does now, was self-protection and protection of the tribe. If humans encountered danger, such as a predator in our midst, the stress reaction was triggered and we were primed to run away, to hide, or to fight to protect ourselves against the life-threatening situation. This protective mechanism is still hard-wired in us in much the same way as it was in primitive times. We are equipped with finely tuned mechanisms to anticipate and prepare for imminent danger. We want to be able to predict and have certainty in our environment, in order to be able to protect.

Imagine you are a cave-person leaving your cave, unable to see around the corner. Something might be lurking there, ready to pounce. Your brain is the tool that anticipates this to keep you safe. But here's the challenge: in real life you live in an era of disruption with an intensification of uncertainty. The world is in a constant state of change, and the predictable movements through life belong to a bygone era. You are no longer in fight or flight to prepare yourself for encounters with tigers or crocodiles. Instead, you are in fight or flight with uncertainty.

This is where the difficulty lies. In an attempt to grapple with uncertainty, you engage in a mental process that ends up having the opposite effect to its intended purpose (more of which later). This mental process is worry.

You are in the boxing ring – and what are you fighting?

Worry is your struggle with the 'what ifs'. Worry is *perceived* threat – a focus on all the possible things that might go wrong. The challenge with worry is that it is a pursuit of certainty when there is no certainty. Rather than sit with the discomfort of uncertainty, you struggle, you grapple, you fight to get certainty or you run away. Your brain is simply not designed to sit comfortably with uncertainty.

The problem is that the fight or flight reaction doesn't just get triggered in response to a real threat; it also gets triggered in response to a *perceived* threat – a worry thought. Your brain sets your body up to fight or to run away in much the same way as for a real threat. Worry triggers a surge of adrenaline and cortisol in your bloodstream; it is this neurochemical reaction that you experience as anxiety or stress. You may breathe more quickly, your heart may pound or you may feel sick or light-headed. But rather than fighting a real threat, you are fighting against the voice of worry, the bully in your mind that alerts you to all the bad things that might happen in the future.

Worry is your inherent desire to self-protect, predict and shape the world around you in order to have certainty, control and safety from any perceived threat. Uncertainty – the 'what if' – is your 'uber' threat. Where there is uncertainty, there is the possibility that something bad might happen, so you fight it, struggle with it and try to get rid of it – and you engage in all sorts of mental and physical behaviours to avoid it. Let's think about our case studies and how they fought with uncertainty.

Case Studies

Ella and Allie both struggled with uncertainty concerning how other people felt about them. Ella questioned whether she would be judged negatively in her family's and colleagues' eyes. She placed unrealistic perfectionistic standards on herself, because where there is perfection there is no uncertainty.

Allie grappled with the uncertainty of what others would think about her in social situations. She feared that they would think she was overweight or ugly and different. She had a specific fear about blushing, as she was concerned that others would judge her in a negative way. Anxious at the thought of not knowing, Allie second-guessed what others were thinking in order to create a greater sense of certainty, but her desire for certainty was never alleviated – and this tipped her into a spiral of worry.

Adam was also at the mercy of uncertainty. The perceived threat, or 'tiger' in Adam's midst, was the fear of failure, or the fear of making a mistake in his schoolwork. His attempts to foresee what would happen with his exams never brought clarity, instead keeping him trapped in anxiety.

Mike had similar concerns. Fear of uncertainty was wreaking havoc in his life. He feared what would happen with his finances and with his health and wellbeing. There was no immediate real threat; it was just the perceived threat, the fear that something bad might happen in the future. In order to alleviate uncertainty from his life, Mike checked excessively – on the internet for health-related symptoms to make sure nothing was wrong with him, and the stock market to make sure he would avoid stupid decisions. In fact, due to his fear of making the wrong decision, he avoided making decisions entirely. His fear of uncertainty trapped him in inertia, which he found hard to escape.

Luke also feared uncertainty. He feared that there would be a dog around the corner that might attack; he feared the uncertainty that smaller dogs would nip him at a moment's notice. He perpetually sought reassurance from his parents to make sure that nothing bad would happen. He felt he just had to know with certainty that he and his family would be safe.

How your brain responds to a worry thought

Your brain responds to a worry thought as if it were a real threat – as if you were being chased or backed into a cave by a tiger. As a result, the prefrontal cortex, which is responsible for your thoughts, beliefs and perception of the world, sets up a connection with the amygdala in the limbic system of the brain to say that something dangerous is happening.

As the primitive stress reaction of flight or fight is triggered, the survival mechanism is now working overtime. Your brain gets 'hijacked' by the amygdala – the part of it that sets up your body to self-protect – to fight or to run. You are overtaken by anxiety, anger or stress, and you can no longer think straight.

Have you ever been getting all stressed out and someone has told you to 'just calm down'? What happens to you in that moment? Typically, it's pretty challenging to just calm down, right? This is the amygdala hijack in action. The amygdala has set up your body to be primed and ready to pounce or to

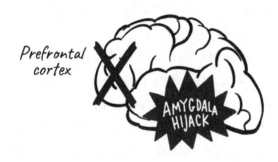

run. In that moment, your brain is not responding to the rationality of 'just calm down' – it's thinking that if it just calms down, an imminent threat will attack. We've all experienced this – it's one of those 'part of being human' things. It's completely and absolutely normal. All the amygdala wants in that moment is to be heard. It is there to protect you and if it isn't heard and is instead being told to switch off, it's going to fire even louder.

To alert you to the possibility of danger, you get a surge of neurochemicals through your bloodstream, such as adrenaline, noradrenaline and cortisol, to set up your body to attack or to run. This rush of neurochemicals is what you experience as anxiety or stress.

The problem with the amygdala hijack in these moments is that you're fighting against a perceived threat, not a real threat – you are fighting against the voice of worry, and so the surge of adrenaline, cortisol and noradrenaline serves no purpose other than whooshing around in your bloodstream.

But your amygdala isn't the enemy. It's just like one of those annoying car alarms that keeps going off when it doesn't need to; it is a little like a friend who gives bad advice from time to time. You have to know when not to get caught up in the alarm bell, but to recognise that it is, in fact, a false alarm. This is when you need the capacity for self-awareness and the tools and techniques to turn the alarm off and to get on with the things you want to get on with – what I call 'heart-driven' purposeful actions rather than fear-driven responses.

What does anxiety feel like in your body?

A great starting point for developing self-awareness is getting to know and understand the feelings of anxiety in your body. It's important to realise that anxiety itself isn't the enemy but, rather, an incredibly helpful physiological reaction in times of real threat.

These physiological experiences present themselves in a variety of ways. And while they are useful when you genuinely need them, they can feel unpleasant, awful and downright terrifying when they are just occurring in response to a worry thought, or a nondescript sense that something bad is about to happen. Having all that adrenaline in your system with nowhere to go can feel physically and emotionally painful and overwhelming.

The reaction begins when a worry thought sends a message to the amygdala, causing an adrenaline surge to rush through your bloodstream and make your heart beat more quickly. As a result, you experience rapid, shallow breathing. This enables blood to be pumped into your large muscle groups to oxygenate them and to help you to fight as effectively as possible or run away as fast as you can. As the blood moves towards your large muscle groups and away from your periphery, you may experience tingly feelings in your fingers and toes. You may also feel dizzy or light-headed as your blood pressure rises.

In addition to this, you might get 'butterflies' in your stomach as the blood rushes out of your stomach – towards your arms and legs. You might experience diarrhoea as the digestive system works less effectively to save energy; the chemicals in your bloodstream might also make you need to go urinate, which helps you to 'lighten your load' so you can be nimble on your feet and fight or run with agility. Your muscles also become tenser, so you can be ready to pounce or protect yourself if attacked. You might even experience a tension headache as your muscles tighten up.

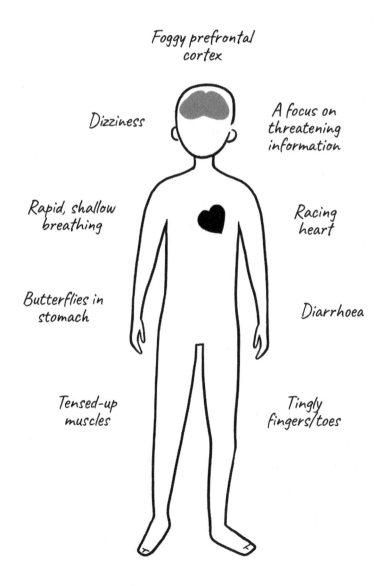

Foggy prefrontal cortex

Dizziness

A focus on threatening information

Rapid, shallow breathing

Racing heart

Butterflies in stomach

Diarrhoea

Tensed-up muscles

Tingly fingers/toes

When you are hijacked by the amygdala, you are locked into the sympathetic nervous system. When your sympathetic nervous system is activated, the subcortical brain structures are primed to override your prefrontal cortex and allow you to respond on instinct. Your cortex, or the part of your brain responsible for rational thoughts and beliefs, becomes less accessible. This accounts for the 'brain fog' that many people experience when they are anxious. Do you feel like you're just unable to think straight when you are experiencing anxiety? This makes sense in the case of a real threat, because the last thing you would want if you were in a life-or-death situation is for your mind to be cluttered by thoughts that are not necessary for your survival. For example, if you were being chased by a tiger, it wouldn't be helpful if you were preoccupied with thoughts such as *What should I wear to the party tonight?* or *What will I make the family for dinner?* If your mind were cluttered by miscellaneous thoughts in that moment, you would end up being dinner!

So, when your prefrontal cortex starts to shut down, it becomes difficult to think clearly. You begin to engage with a fight or flight mindset and your capacity for rational and reflective thinking becomes limited. Sometimes people might feel like they are going crazy or 'losing their mind'.

This all starts to make a lot more sense when you understand that anxiety is just your body responding to a perceived threat (a worry thought) as if it were a real threat (a tiger), and that all your primitive neural mechanisms of survival are telling you to do is to fight or to run. The sympathetic nervous system and the neurochemicals of the fight or flight reaction are mutually exclusive from the calming and quietening neurochemicals of the parasympathetic nervous system. At a basic neurochemical level, oxytocin, the hormone responsible for attachment and cohesion; melatonin, the hormone responsible for sleep onset; and serotonin, the hormone responsible for staying calm and 'chilled', have all shut down.

When your brain locks you into your sympathetic nervous system and your oxytocin shuts down, it impacts your capacity to have cohesive and connected relationships. Instead, you might be more inclined to disengage, or become agitated, avoidant, argumentative or aggressive.

Further to this, as melatonin, responsible for sleep onset, shuts down, you don't fall asleep, or if you wake up, you find it hard to get back to sleep. (If you think about it, the last thing you want to do when you are being chased by a tiger is to fall asleep or fall in love!) Instead, the adrenaline and cortisol in your veins keep you awake. And when your sleep deteriorates and you disengage from others, your relationships can break down, you can get bowled over by agitation, and a negative spiral kicks in.

The good news is you're going to learn how you can get out of the amygdala hijack when it's happening. I'm here to equip you with strategies that you can use to help yourself, and your loved ones, in the best way at these critical times.

Hypervigilance to threat-relevant information

Let's look at another physiological reaction that occurs with worry. Your brain is wired to focus in on what you feel threatened by – this is called 'hypervigilance to threat-relevant information'. This means the fight or flight reaction makes you preoccupied with the source of the threat; you focus on any information associated with what you feel threatened by – to ensure that you don't miss anything that might harm you! The problem is that if your source of threat is simply your worry thoughts, you find yourself focusing in on these thoughts and it becomes difficult to quieten your mind.

Let's think about an example of hypervigilance to threat in action. Imagine you are going on a bushwalk. What might you see around you? Perhaps birds, trees or insects. What might you hear around you? Perhaps the sound of leaves or sticks under your feet, the sound of the wind, or wildlife. What might you smell around you? Perhaps the fresh air or the damp foliage.

Now, just say a metre and a half in front of you, you see a red-bellied black snake. NOW what are you seeing? That's right – the snake! NOW what are you hearing? That's right – the snake! NOW what are you smelling? That's right – the snake!

All of your senses focus in on the snake. Why? Because the snake is your threat and your brain is programmed to focus in on danger. It is important for your survival.

The problem is your brain responds to a worry thought, a perceived threat, as if it were a real threat – like a red-bellied black snake. It focuses in on the worry thought, and anything to do with the worry thought. The difficult part about this is you then notice the bad stuff more, or your imagination works overtime and makes you think that bad stuff is happening when you have no real evidence.

As another example, let's say you have a fear of spiders. You might be more likely to scan the corners of the room as you walk in, or more likely to tune in to reports to do with spiders when you listen to the news. As a result, your perceived frequency of bad things happening to do with spiders is greater, thereby keeping you trapped in your fear.

Consider how hypervigilance is playing out in your life

Let's look at how worry can increase your perceived likelihood of something bad happening. Consider the following questions:

- What specific fears might you have?
- What is worry telling you?
- Do you find that your brain tends to pick up on stories that relate to those things just a little more?
- Do you scan for information in social or interpersonal situations so you are prepared if something bad were to happen?
- Do you potentially avoid those situations in the first place, just in case?

For now, just write these observations down. Later, I'll show you how you can shift from fear and avoidance behaviours to resilience and positive action.

Think about how hypervigilance to threat played out in the lives of our case studies.

Allie noticed any sign of when she was potentially left out of social arrangements or if people weren't smiling at her at a party. She second-guessed herself and created all sorts of stories in her mind about what others were thinking, inevitably negative stories about her friends thinking she was ugly, fat or a loser. Because it is impossible to know what somebody else is thinking, Allie had to base her assumptions on the sensory cues available. The problem, as we now know, is that our brain is wired to focus in on what we feel threatened by. So Allie misinterpreted ambiguous cues such as people talking quietly to one another, and assumed they were talking about her.

Hypervigilance to threat-relevant information plays out clearly in cases of specific phobias. Luke's fear of dogs set his brain up to be acutely aware of any news stories about dog attacks in the community. He scanned the park for dogs, noticing even the smallest dog on the furthest side of the field. His ears would prick up if a dog was ever mentioned in a conversation among his friends. He interpreted the facial expressions of the dogs he saw on his computer or television as more menacing and 'angry' than did other family members. He even took a dislike to the colour brown because of its association with dogs.

Hypervigilance to threat also created a challenge with Mike's health anxiety. His brain was acutely aware of any physiological changes in his body. He scanned and checked it regularly to make sure that nothing bad was happening. As a result, he noticed when there were any new pains, protrusions, spots or sensations. Like Luke, Mike also picked up on any negative stories on the news about cancer or pollutants in the environment making people more susceptible to illness, thus reinforcing his fears. He searched the internet regularly, finding confirmation that his physiological sensations might indicate something catastrophic. There was always doubt and the doubt was reinforced by hypervigilance.

The negativity bias

The other challenge when it comes to our brain programming is our inherent negativity bias. Humans are not typically positive thinkers. If you think about more primitive times when things were either a friend and would sustain us, or a foe and would kill us, our brain was wired to seek out the negatives to protect us. We were more inclined to look out for the tigers lurking in the bushes than the butterflies in the field. We still have largely the same neural wiring – in an ambiguous situation, human beings are more likely to interpret cues negatively, thereby triggering the primitive threat instinct.

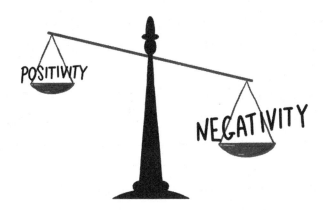

The negativity bias plays out in many varied circumstances in our lives. For example, it might be particularly prominent when you have a work presentation you are about to give, an exam you are studying for or an event you are going to. Your brain is wired to tip to focusing on the outcome – and it is not a bed of roses that the human brain is programmed to see. We see stuff-ups. We see criticism. We see failure.

But aren't I supposed to just think positively?

Does this sound familiar? Has anybody ever said to you, 'Just stop being so negative! Why can't you just focus on the positives?' Or perhaps you've read one of those self-help books that instructs you to tell yourself positive things and you will become more positive. Has this worked? Sure, there will be times that hopefulness kicks in and you say, 'Right, now I'm going to absolutely try this positive thinking thing.' You practise really, really hard. But what happens? Worry butts in. You say, 'Yes, I'm going to do really well in this test!' and worry says, 'No, you're not.' So you then say, 'Yes, yes, I am going to do well!' and worry responds, 'But what if you don't?' So you seek reassurance, you check in with your partner, your friends, your parents. You start to over-check your work just in case. And then the spiral unravels – worry has hooked you in.

The fact is that positive thinking runs counter to the way our brain is wired. Human beings just aren't inherently positive. Arguing with your negative or worry thoughts to 'just think positively', to 'just be happy' – to discount the negatives – actually sets you up for letting yourself down right from the beginning. It typically isn't all that helpful.

In fact, paradoxically, it makes anxiety worse. It gets you focusing in on the worry and all the possible things that might go wrong. Worry will pipe up and point out something bad that could happen. You then get caught up in the boxing ring with worry, and you end up digging yourself in deeper. It might be a helpful way to alleviate the anxiety and stress in the moment, but anxiety has a habit of creeping back in. This is called a safety behaviour (I talk about this more in Chapter 12). It is different from practising strategies such as focusing on things that you feel grateful for, which is a powerful and scientifically supported mood booster (see pages 232 and 287 for more about gratitude).

The negativity bias was particularly challenging for Adam. His family valued achievement and he truly wanted to succeed; however, he feared that he wasn't good enough and dreaded approaching assignments or studying for exams. His mind tipped to focusing on the outcomes, and he could see himself sitting in the exam room and freezing up. He found his homework boring and difficult – and thought the teacher wouldn't be satisfied anyway. A brick wall started to build up every time he approached his work. His brain interpreted that the outcome would be a disaster, so he had better avoid it to be safe.

Ella had a strong negativity bias in her self-perceptions at home and at work. She felt so strongly that she would fail, she believed herself to be a fraud in her work environment. Despite experiencing a succession of promotions over the years and receiving positive approval from others, Ella still felt like she was a university student and not worthy of the praise and success she had achieved. She focused on the negatives about herself and feared failure in the future to the point that she believed it to be true. Ella was stuck in a vicious cycle brought about by the negativity bias, among other patterns typical of anxiety. This created a phenomenon known as imposter syndrome, an anxiety challenge driven by a fear of not being good enough and a fear of negative judgement.

Think about whether something similar plays out in your own mind. Do you have an inner voice telling you you're not good enough? Perhaps it convinces you that you are a fraud and that you don't deserve the good experiences that come your way. I share strategies to help you to stand up to this critical voice, which caring human beings so commonly experience, in Chapter 22.

How does anxiety differ from fear?

I'm often asked how the experience of anxiety is different from the experience of fear. Fear occurs when there is an imminent threat from a known source of danger, and defence or avoidance of the danger is required immediately. For example, you might be driving and witness another car out of control. A specific and immediate urge to act is required and fear propels you into action. Anxiety, on the other hand, occurs in response to a vague or unknown perceived threat. It is a longer-lasting emotional state of nervousness or apprehension that puts you on alert to a future threat or to the possibility of danger.

Chapter 6

Understanding anxiety

Make it your friend
and find freedom

Now that we've explored the neuroscience of anxiety a little more closely, you can see that it is a critically important friend in times of need. You don't want to hate anxiety. You want to understand it, respect it, and leverage it at times when it keeps you fired up, alert and responding effectively.

Ultimately, the purpose of anxiety is to help you to pay attention and to provide the energy to act. It is prevalent in all humans and commonly prevalent in the most caring of individuals; it is a deep desire to protect. So recognise that anxiety is a double-edged sword. Anxiety might feel uncomfortable, which is exactly the purpose it is serving – it is there to motivate you towards action in order to remove the unpleasant feeling. For example, you might feel anxious when you are finalising a work project, and once the task is completed the anxiety disappears. Anxiety in and of itself is, therefore, a critically important thing – a physiological reaction to propel you towards self-protection and getting things done.

In fact, along the way, it was the non-anxious people who were eaten by the tigers – which is perhaps another reason why humans today are susceptible to being anxious. You are a descendant of the ones who survived – the ones who had an active amygdala, which kept them alive long enough to procreate. A simplistic conceptualisation is to think of us as the descendants of the neurotic apes, because the happy-go-lucky apes were eaten by the sabre-toothed tigers!

When you can observe the anxiety feelings in your body and understand that they are, in fact, your body trying to help you, it can help you to feel less anxious about being anxious.

The sensations you feel throughout your body all make sense in the context of setting up your body to defend itself, or run away, in a threatening situation. But if you don't understand what these sensations are, you may think they mean that something bad is happening and that you need to respond by working out a way to avoid the situation or protect yourself.

Alternatively, you might experience these sensations and think that something catastrophic is happening inside your body and you become anxious about being anxious. This is what happens when an individual experiences a panic attack. You feel all these horrible feelings in your body, which are indeed benign, but instead you might think ...

I don't like these feelings.
These feelings are scaring me.
They must mean something disastrous is happening
*   in my body.*
They must mean I am going to die.

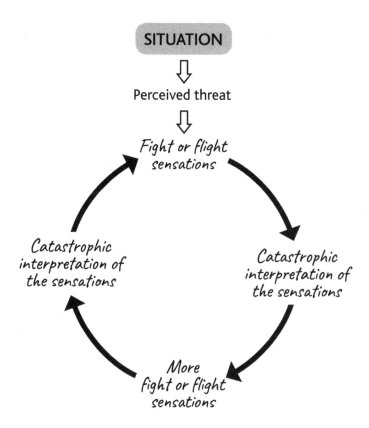

SITUATION

⇩

Perceived threat

⇩

Fight or flight sensations

Catastrophic interpretation of the sensations

Catastrophic interpretation of the sensations

More fight or flight sensations

Now, you cannot definitively say that nothing bad is happening – you will never have certainty. However, when you instead sit with the discomfort of uncertainty and respond to the experiences with self-awareness, you build greater acceptance around the experience of anxiety and take yourself out of fight or flight. As a result, you circumvent the panic cycle and end up feeling better.

So understanding what the fight or flight reaction is can be incredibly helpful. Remember that the amygdala, or the control centre of the fight or flight reaction, is a friend who gives you bad advice from time to time. You might find yourself in stressful situations where the amygdala feels like it's running on over-drive. Your power will come from choosing how you respond.

This is the essence of the Mind Strength Method. Alongside the ability to build awareness around worry, anxiety and fear, and the ability to build awareness around values, goals and actions, is a toolkit to build resilience. If you follow these steps, the fight or flight reaction loosens its grip and your own empowerment takes over.

MIND STRENGTH ACTION

Explore your feelings of anxiety

Think about the last few times that you felt anxious:

- What were the situations when anxiety came up for you?
- What were some of the thoughts?
- Now think about the sensations of anxiety. Where did the anxiety sensations show up in your body? See if you can pinpoint them.
- Can you put words to your experiences?
- Can you start to explore those feelings with a little more self-awareness and understanding of what they are?

Take a moment to draw an outline of yourself on a piece of paper. It can be helpful to colour the parts of your body where the anxiety shows up and write some words about the experiences. As you do that, can you practise responding to those feelings with kindness, love, appreciation and care, rather than hating, struggling and fighting with them? Start to breathe through those feelings and experiment with the practice of noticing them, observing them, allowing them and understanding them.

For now, see if you can experiment with changing your relationship with anxiety and start to make friends with it. When you no longer perceive it as a threat, and no longer get anxious about being anxious, you are already on the path towards freedom.

Pivoting from threat perception to positive action

Alongside understanding anxiety, your perception of a situation is critical in determining the emotion you experience in that situation. Depending on whether you are focused on your threats or focused on your values and goals (we'll go into this in Chapter 16), the adrenaline response that propels you towards action might show up as a whole realm of different emotions that are experienced as either positive or negative.

For example, you could perceive a situation as threatening, driven by a run of worry thoughts that tell you something bad might happen in the future. This triggers the amygdala hijack and a negative experience of anxiety. A work project may be viewed as a threat if you focus on your perceived 'not good enoughs' and feared negative outcomes, underpinned by worry thoughts such as ...

What if I fail?
What if I'm not good enough?
What if they reject my proposal?

And those worry thoughts could result in delay, avoidance, upset and probably a poor outcome. Or you might perceive that same situation as a heart-driven goal that you are working towards. You could focus on your effort and what you do well, which will, in turn, propel you towards positive action. The same situation might be underpinned by thoughts such as ...

This is an exciting opportunity.
I'm going to give this my very best effort.
This situation is an interesting challenge.

In this case, the energy and motivation towards action is more likely to be associated with a positive emotional experience of drive, enthusiasm or excitement.

This helpful and motivational purpose of anxiety has typically been obscured by the negative perception of the emotion. The way you perceive the situation will determine whether the emotion is positive or negative. Typically, moderate amounts of adrenaline accompanied by a focus on values and goals facilitate high performance and more positive mood states. Excitement can produce a level of arousal, an intense focus on a project and the experience of being 'in the zone'. This motivational element of anxiety is helpful, adaptive and at times critical, in response to a real need to get something done.

Different emotional experiences may play out as follows:

- If you are relying on others to do a task and the things that need to be achieved are not being done, you might experience anger, agitation or frustration.

- If you have many things to get done and little time to do them, the emotion you experience might be distress, annoyance or despair.
- If the fight or flight reaction is driven by something that you want to repel or avoid because it is perceived as revolting or repulsive, the emotion experienced might be disgust.
- If the fight or flight reaction is activated due to the perceived potential of humiliation or failure, the emotion that might be experienced is guilt or shame.

In all cases, anxiety provides the adrenaline to act. What tips anxiety into overdrive is your mindset – whether you focus on your threats or focus on your goals, and how you choose to perceive the situation in any given moment.

Pivoting out of threat perception and towards purpose, values and goals is the essence of the Mind Strength Method. For example, let's consider someone with anxiety about their health. This would mean pivoting away from worry about the possibility of something bad happening (leading to negativity bias, over-checking and hypervigilance to the threat) towards problem-solving and goal-driven actions for maintaining a balanced, healthy lifestyle. In a business setting, this might be helping individuals to shift from worry about the possible things that might go wrong in the future towards identifying the business's strategic direction and implementing team alignment on organisational values and goals.

Tip the focus from your head to your heart

Perhaps some challenging thoughts came up yesterday or the day before. Perhaps a critical voice is telling you that you're not good enough or that you'll be rejected. Try to experiment with pivoting away from the head to the heart:

- See if you can recall the worry story that has been playing in your mind. Did you try to struggle with those thoughts? Did you try to block them and get rid of them? Perhaps you found yourself hooked into a worry snowball that began to grow.

- Now see if you can tip the focus away from your head, and the second-guessing, questioning, self-doubting or fear-driven story that might be playing there, and towards your heart. What direction do you want to move towards? This is the heart-driven pull.

- Can you think about 'heart-driven pull towards' actions associated with this (empowered or assertive actions, for example) rather than 'fear-driven push away from' actions (over-checking or people-pleasing, for example)?

In Part 3, I will share a Mind Strength Toolkit with you to bring this pivot well and truly within your grasp. For now, I encourage you to explore the experiences that come up for you. Notice if there are any differences in the emotions that play out in that small moment, and experiment with the pivot from pushing away from fear to pulling towards heart-driven action.

The Mind Strength Method is built on the premise that you can create space to tip the focus away from your worry thoughts and perceived threats, which exist in your mind, and towards your heart-space (see opposite) or your values, and the things that provide you with a sense of meaning, purpose and fulfilment. You experience the worry and fear-driven thoughts as the *push away from* something bad that might happen, and the values-driven heart-space as the *pull towards* a desired direction. It's not an attempt to get rid of the worry thoughts, because that will just end up making the worry thoughts stronger. Rather, it's your ability to notice the worry thoughts, to acknowledge them, to even say hello to them, and then refocus on your values.

What is emotional intelligence?

Emotional intelligence is awareness of emotions in yourself and others. It is the ability to regulate your emotions and remain calm through challenge, rather than being led astray by the voice of worry or anger and the hijacking amygdala. Emotional intelligence is your ability to evaluate the situation, to adapt your behaviour and respond effectively, ensuring your alignment with purpose, values and goals. Emotional intelligence enables you to know what you are feeling, what your emotions mean, how these emotions can affect other people, and the ability to adapt your emotions and behaviour accordingly.

Case Study

Mike was experiencing significant struggles with his emotions. Worry had led to him being overwhelmed by fear-driven actions, such as checking and rechecking his work and second-guessing himself in professional situations. His mind was racing in overdrive. He found it difficult to get to sleep and was also waking up in the early hours, typically around 3 am, with a whirlwind of thoughts and intermittently in a state of panic. These experiences were tipping Mike into low mood, anxiety, agitation and aggression.

Mike found that he had an uncharacteristically short fuse. Anger started to take hold and situations would trigger him to fire back unwittingly at others, both in work and personal contexts. He felt that he had lost control of his emotions, and it was undermining his capacity to engage effectively. Reflecting and calming down in the moment before acting was proving tricky, and the more his emotions got the better of him, the more he became frazzled and unhinged.

Anxiety, low mood, agitation and stress had reduced Mike's capacity for emotionally intelligent interactions at home and at work. He recognised that the emotional outbursts were undermining his ability to live his life how he wanted to live it. They were eroding the most precious relationships he had, those with his wife and his children. Mike had a deep desire to learn how to manage anxiety and boost his mood, and he also wanted to learn how to build awareness of his emotions and regain control of them. He wanted the flexibility to adapt his emotions in times of distress and forge meaningful, effective connections with those around him.

Chapter 7

The difference between anxiety and an anxiety disorder

*When anxiety causes prolonged fear,
suffering and avoidance, it is defined
as an anxiety disorder*

Hopefully, you are already sitting even the slightest bit more comfortably knowing that anxiety is an essential part of being human and something that is hard-wired in all of us. Anxiety is not weird, a weakness or something to feel ashamed of – it is a completely normal and helpful reaction when you need it.

I conceptualise anxiety as a continuum. We all experience different levels of anxiety. This is due to factors such as genetic makeup, temperament, family history, brain functioning and neurochemistry, personal experiences and the interplay across them all. Some medical conditions are also known to cause or exacerbate feelings of anxiety, so it's always a good idea to see a medical doctor if you are experiencing an increase in anxiety symptoms.

Recall too the double-edged sword of anxiety. Often individuals who experience anxiety are analytical thinkers who feel emotions at a deeper level and have higher levels of empathy. In fact, part of conquering anxiety is recognising the inherent qualities and strengths in these characteristics that you possess while standing up to the challenges. You want to accept and change your relationship with the anxiety and truly understand it for what it is. This understanding of anxiety is core to Step 1 of the Mind Strength Method. When you no longer fight anxiety but rather accept and change your relationship with it, you've made the first fundamental step in moving from anxiety to effective, empowered action.

When does anxiety become an anxiety disorder?

Anxiety that is part of our common human experience tips over into an anxiety disorder when worry persists over time and causes prolonged fear, suffering and avoidance in your personal, professional or academic life. The consistent features across all anxiety disorders include worry, nervousness and fear that are ongoing, excessive and get in the way of your ability to function as you would otherwise want to.

Commonly, people experiencing clinical anxiety have symptoms across more than one anxiety disorder and can experience mood-related challenges as well. The relationship between anxiety and depression is often bidirectional, where anxiety can detrimentally impact mood and low mood can exacerbate anxiety. Due to the frequent co-occurrence of anxiety and depression, and the fact that improving mood helps to conquer anxiety, powerful and scientifically supported mood boosters are an important tool in the Mind Strength Method (see Chapter 21).

Anxiety disorder symptoms may not go away on their own and, if left untreated, can get worse over time. So, if you are suffering from worry and anxiety that are causing prolonged fear, suffering and avoidance in your life, it is a good idea to seek help from a clinical psychologist or other mental health professional specifically trained in scientifically supported treatment strategies for clinical anxiety. There is no stigma or shame in experiencing anxiety, so please do seek out the help you need.

When choosing a mental health professional, it is important to note that while talking therapy can help you to work through problems and determine action plans, help for anxiety typically requires strategies specifically for managing clinical anxiety, such as the cognitive and behavioural interventions described in this book. Talking therapy alone is generally not sufficient to help remedy the challenges of clinical anxiety. The good news is that with the right evidence-based strategies, anxiety problems can be remedied quickly. The Mind Strength Method is a proven methodology for treating anxiety disorders and will equip you with a practical and effective Mind Strength Toolkit for life.

There are three main classes of anxiety-related disorders, and these are described on the following pages.

1. Anxiety disorders

Anxiety disorders are characterised by excessive fear, suffering and avoidance in a person's life due to a perceived threat, and the associated fear of adverse behavioural and emotional consequences. Anxiety disorders differ from normal feelings of nervousness or anxiousness due to the excessive and prolonged nature of the fear. Anxiety disorders are the most common of the mental health issues, affecting nearly 25 per cent of the population at some point in their lives. Some of the more frequent presentations of anxiety disorders are described below.

Generalised anxiety disorder

The hallmark feature of generalised anxiety disorder (GAD) is excessive worry on most days for a period of six months or more.

Intermittent anxiety and worry are normal and common parts of life, particularly if you experience a stressful life event, such as taking an examination, public speaking or attending a job interview. This is when anxiety can keep you alert and focused and help you get things done quickly and at your best. However, individuals diagnosed with GAD experience anxiety and worry most of the time rather than just in specific stressful situations. The worries are intense, persistent and get in the way of normal functioning.

The content of the worries might relate to several aspects of everyday life, such as health, finances, work and family. Even small aspects of life, such as washing clothes or being late for a meeting, can become the focus of anxiety, resulting in overwhelming worries and a feeling of impending catastrophe. Specifically, a GAD diagnosis is warranted if, for more days than not over a period of six months, you have experienced

- worry impacting your ability to do everyday activities such as studying, going to work, or catching up with family and friends
- excessive worry
- difficulty stopping worrying, and
- worrying about more than one activity

As well as three or more of the following symptoms:

- feeling restless or on edge
- feeling easily fatigued
- difficulty concentrating
- feeling irritable
- muscle tension
- restless sleep, difficulty falling asleep or staying asleep.

Social anxiety disorder

Social anxiety disorder is diagnosed if you have an intense fear of being judged negatively, embarrassed, laughed at, humiliated or criticised in everyday situations.

While it is normal and common to feel somewhat nervous or anxious in social and interpersonal situations, particularly when you are interacting with or being watched by others, for individuals with social anxiety disorder even everyday performance or social situations can trigger intense anxiety.

Anxiety can show up in many ways. You may find yourself

- worrying excessively about the perceived consequences of doing or saying the wrong thing
- avoiding situations where there is a fear of acting in a particular humiliating or embarrassing way. This may result in missing school, work or social activities
- enduring situations with dread if avoidance isn't possible, and attempting to escape the situation quickly or to numb the anxiety through various means such as alcohol or recreational drugs.

The symptoms must be persistent for at least six months for a diagnosis to be made. Anxiety might be triggered in the lead-up to, or during, a social or performance situation. The social anxiety can relate to either a specific situation or many varied situations. Examples include

- meeting unfamiliar people
- eating or drinking in public or in front of others
- talking on the phone
- performing in front of others, such as giving a speech or a presentation
- making conversation
- being assertive in social, school or work situations.

Both physical and psychological symptoms are common with social anxiety. The physical symptoms can be distressing to individuals and include shaking, blushing, perspiration, stuttering, nausea and diarrhoea. There is intense self-focused awareness (hypervigilance) on the specific physical symptoms experienced. The fear of other people seeing them further exacerbates the anxiety, even though the signs might be hardly visible to others.

Due to attempts to avoid the feared situations, social anxiety can significantly impact personal and professional relationships and day-to-day experiences, such as seeing family and friends, studying and going to work.

Specific phobia

While fear of a dangerous situation is a normal and adaptive response to protect yourself from a real threat, a specific phobia is a persistent, excessive and unreasonable fear of a specific object, activity, animal or situation. A specific phobia interferes with daily life, such as being able to work, study or see family or friends, and persists for at least six months.

Concern or fear about specific situations, activities, animals or objects is a common occurrence. For example, many people feel nervous about snakes, spiders, heights or plane travel. For a specific phobia to be diagnosed, individuals must react to objects, activities or situations by exaggerating the perceived danger. Panic or terror is out of proportion to the level of actual threat. A person might go to great lengths to try to avoid certain situations for fear of the possibility of facing the dreaded stimulus, such as not going to a park because there might be a dog, changing work patterns or avoiding a health check-up. High levels of distress might be triggered if the specific situation or object is unavoidable. If you have a specific phobia, you might recognise that your reaction is irrational or exaggerated but feel like you just can't help it.

Specific phobias are divided into fears related to

- animals (e.g. dogs or spiders)
- natural environment (e.g. thunder or heights)
- blood, injection or injury (e.g. needles, sight of blood)
- specific situations (e.g. elevators, bridges, driving, flying)
- other specific phobia (e.g. choking, vomiting).

The specific phobia can trigger a panic attack, which is an acute onset of intense, overwhelming and perceived uncontrollable feelings of anxiety accompanied by extreme physical sensations of the fight or flight reaction, including a racing heart, tightness in the chest, a sense of choking, nausea, dizziness, feeling hot or sweating. At times, just the thought of the source of the threat or seeing it on a computer, television or in a book can trigger the fear response.

Panic disorder

Panic disorder is diagnosed when a person repeatedly experiences panic attacks. The attacks are often unexpected and experienced as if they came 'out of the blue'. The individual may think that they are having a heart attack or are about to die.

For a diagnosis of panic disorder to be made, the individual must have recurrent, disabling panic attacks, or have persistent fears of having a panic attack, for a period of one month or more. The person might also worry that the panic attack is a sign of an undiagnosed medical health problem and fear the consequences of the attack. The fear persists, which can lead to repeated medical tests and prolonged hypervigilance to try to determine the underlying physiological cause, despite reassurance.

If you have experienced more than four of the physical symptoms below for one month or more and have also felt persistently worried about experiencing these feelings again, or if you have changed your behaviour to try to avoid having panic attacks, you may be experiencing panic disorder. Panic attacks symptoms include

- a sense of overwhelming panic or fear
- the thought that you are dying, choking, 'losing control' or 'going mad'
- increased heart rate
- feeling that there is not enough air
- feeling like you are choking
- excessive perspiration
- depersonalisation or feeling detached from yourself or your surroundings
- a lump in the throat
- trembling or shaking
- a racing heart
- shortness of breath
- feeling nauseous or having butterflies or pain in your stomach
- feeling dizzy, light-headed or faint
- feeling numb or tingly
- a sense that you or the world around you is not real

- hot or cold flushes
- fear of losing control or going crazy
- fear of dying.

Panic attacks are fairly common. Up to 40 per cent of the population will experience a panic attack at some point in their life. Panic attacks reach a peak within about 10 minutes and usually last for up to half an hour, which can leave an individual feeling exhausted. They can occur several times a day or may happen only once every few years. They can even occur while people are asleep, waking them up at night.

2. Obsessive compulsive and related disorders

Obsessive compulsive and related disorders are characterised by obsessive, intrusive and repetitive worrying thoughts, images or urges. These trigger related mental and physical compulsive behaviours, or activities that are done in a repeated or ordered way, to neutralise the associated anxiety or distress (e.g. washing, cleaning, arranging, checking, eating). There is relief experienced in the short term by engaging in the compulsions; however, the anxiety is soon felt again, resulting in the need to repeat the actions.

Typically, our thoughts are helpful and influence our behaviour in adaptive ways, such as when we wonder whether we locked the car door and then go back to make sure we did. However, for individuals experiencing OCD, these thoughts, feelings and behaviours are unwanted, unreasonable or excessive, and interfere with normal daily functioning. For example, a preoccupation or obsessive concern regarding whether or not you have locked the door might lead to repeated checking. A person will often acknowledge that these thoughts and behaviours are irrational but find it hard to stop. Another example is a fear of germs and contamination leading to constant washing of hands and clothes.

Obsessions or compulsions or both can be present. Typically, obsessions cluster around certain themes with certain associated compulsive behaviours, including

- an exaggerated fear of contamination, resulting in a need for cleanliness and control – examples of associated compulsive behaviours are washing hands and clothes, showering or brushing teeth, household cleaning including tidying and arranging things
- a need for order or symmetry, resulting in an overwhelming need to perform tasks or place objects, such as books or cutlery, in a particular way
- an obsessive urge to count, resulting in a need to repeatedly count items or objects in a particular way
- hoarding, resulting in a need to retain items such as junk mail and old newspapers
- an obsessive concern regarding body appearance, resulting in compulsions around eating, dieting, appearance and exercise
- a fear of harm occurring to oneself or others, resulting in compulsive behaviours to do with safety, such as checking whether the stove has been turned off, or seeking

reassurance that someone is okay or that the windows and doors are locked
- an obsession regarding sexual identity, resulting in a preoccupation with sexual activity and associated checking, avoidance and reassurance seeking
- obsessive worries regarding religious or moral issues, resulting in compulsions to pray or engage in ritualised activities that interfere with work and relationships.

3. Trauma and stressor related disorders

In trauma and stressor related disorders, anxiety evolves as a byproduct of the experience of a trauma or life stressor. Examples of life stressors include divorce, moving country or beginning university. Examples of trauma might include an unexpected death of a loved one, war, a car accident, assault, a natural disaster or a violent or sudden injury, resulting in you feeling very scared or helpless.

Post-traumatic stress disorder (PTSD) is a particular set of reactions that can develop in people who have been through a traumatic event that threatened their life and safety, or the safety of the people around them. This could be a serious accident, physical or sexual assault, war, torture, or disasters such as bushfires or floods. This can lead to feelings of intense fear or panic, helplessness or horror. A person can feel physically and psychologically distressed when reminded of the event.

PTSD is diagnosed when a person has symptoms clustering around the following areas for at least a month.

- Re-experiencing the traumatic event through unwanted and recurring memories, often in the form of vivid images or flashbacks and nightmares. There might be intense emotional or physical reactions, such as sweating, heart palpitations or panic when reminded of the event.
- Being overly alert or wound up, including difficulty relaxing, difficulty falling asleep or staying asleep, irritability and a short fuse to anger, difficulty concentrating, being easily startled, or being on guard or on the lookout for signs of danger.
- Avoiding reminders of anything related to the event including activities, places, people, thoughts or feelings due to the painful memories they might bring up.
- Feeling emotionally flat or numb, difficulty feeling positive emotions, feeling detached from friends and family or experiencing less interest in day-to-day activities that you used to enjoy.

Other experiences might include

- difficulty remembering parts of the event
- negative beliefs about yourself, others or the world
- persistently blaming yourself or others for what happened
- persistently feeling negative, guilty or ashamed
- reckless or self-destructive behaviour.

The Mind Strength Method has demonstrated effectiveness for the treatment of anxiety disorders and anxiety-related disorders at all levels of severity. There is no need to suffer in silence when the road to freedom from worry, anxiety and fear comes into view – and the road does not have to be long. By embracing the Mind Strength Method and the strategies contained in this book, you are well and truly on your way.

Alongside these strategies, it is also often helpful to work with a trained mental health professional – after all, if you had a toothache, you'd go to the dentist, right? Whether you are suffering from anxiety, general stress, a life crisis or a diagnosable anxiety disorder, there are many highly trained professionals who can help you if you are finding things difficult at work, school or home. Similarly, for some individuals, medication prescribed by a trained medical professional can be helpful. If you are having mental health challenges, it is always advisable to seek guidance from your general practitioner, who is an excellent gatekeeper of medical care and will be familiar with a well-trained mental health professional who can help you.

Chapter 8

What about stress?

Stress is our body's call to action

I'm frequently asked about the difference between anxiety and stress. Both stress and anxiety are our body's physiological reaction to perceived threat in our environment. Stress is typically the term used for our body's immediate response to a demand or threat. The stress response gets activated when we sense danger, whether real or imagined, and the body's defences take hold in the form of the rapid, automatic process of the fight or flight reaction. Anxiety typically involves your thoughts and anticipation of certain bad things happening in the future.

As with anxiety, the stress response in itself isn't a bad thing. It is your body's way of protecting you. In suitable smaller amounts, the stress response helps you to stay focused, energised, alert and able to meet new challenges. In emergency situations, stress can save your life. For example, it might give you the extra strength to defend yourself or help you to react quickly, such as if you need to jump out of the way of a car racing around the corner.

Stress can also help you rise to meet challenges. It is what keeps you alert and on your toes in challenging circumstances, such as a work presentation or needing to meet a deadline. Stress can prevent accidents or costly mistakes by sharpening your concentration when you need it. The technical word for this is 'eustress' or good stress. Typically, with eustress you are focused on your goals, not focused on your threats. It can keep you buoyant, animated and energised. When you feel 'in the zone' or 'pumped' this is typically eustress. It can be the adrenaline needed to stay fired up to get your job done effectively.

Problems arise when stress tips into large amounts over an extended period of time. If you experience too much stress you might feel frazzled, overloaded, exhausted, unappreciated, agitated or over-reactive. Stress that continues without reprieve, or stress that is generated by focusing on your threats, can lead to distress. This is when stress stops being helpful and starts causing problems.

Distress can disturb your body's internal balance and be detrimental to your health, your mood, your relationships, your productivity and your life. Over prolonged periods, cortisol and adrenaline build up in your bloodstream and can disrupt many vital systems in your body, such as your immune system, your digestive system and your reproductive system. Prolonged stress can increase your risk of heart attack and stroke, and can speed up the aging process. With chronic stress, you can start to experience physical symptoms, including headaches, an upset stomach, high blood pressure, chest pain, sexual dysfunction and sleep problems. Emotional problems also evolve from prolonged high stress. These problems might include depression and, you guessed it, anxiety. In fact, scientific research has linked stress to some of the leading causes of death among adults, including heart disease, cancer, lung problems, accidents, cirrhosis of the liver and suicide.

Is it burnout?

The concept of burnout is recognised by the World Health Organization as a problem resulting from chronic or unrelenting high workplace stress that has not been successfully managed. When there's too much stress you might feel overloaded and exhausted but this is not burnout. Typically, if you experience stress, you can still imagine that if you can just get everything under control, your situation will improve. In contrast, when you experience burnout, you typically do not see any hope of positive change in your situation. Burnout is when stress exceeds your ability to cope, causing damage to your mind, body and job satisfaction.

Being burned out results in the experience of feeling empty and mentally exhausted, a total loss of motivation, and going beyond caring. If excessive stress feels like you are drowning in responsibilities, burnout is a sense of total depletion. The challenge is that while you might usually be aware of being under a lot of stress, burnout can creep up on you without you recognising that it is even happening. Burnout is an experience of stress reaching saturation point, with an inability to continue to push through.

Burnout is not considered a mental disorder per se but is recognised as a precursor to mood and anxiety related problems.

The key to the burnout label is that the symptoms specifically occur in the context of the workplace. These symptoms are characterised by

- feelings of energy depletion or exhaustion
- increased emotional disengagement from your job, or negative feelings related to your job
- reduced professional efficacy.

Burnout is a gradual process. The signs and symptoms are subtle at first but become worse as time goes on. Think of the early symptoms as red flags that something is wrong and needs to be addressed. If you pay attention and actively reduce your stress, you can prevent a major breakdown. If you ignore them, you'll eventually burn out.

Some physical signs of burnout include

- reduced immunity, increased illness and stomach problems
- headaches, muscle tension and muscle pain
- changes in appetite and sleep, increased fatigue and difficulty concentrating.

Some emotional signs of burnout include

- sense of failure and self-doubt
- feeling helpless, trapped and defeated
- detachment and feeling alone
- loss of motivation and confidence
- increased cynicism and negative outlook

- decreased satisfaction and sense of accomplishment
- feeling overwhelmed, anxious, angry and irritable
- down, withdrawn, flat emotions and a sense of hopelessness.

Some behavioural signs of burnout include

- withdrawing from responsibilities, disengagement, loss of interest in work, apathy, loss of motivation and hope
- procrastinating and taking longer to get things done
- skipping work, coming in late and leaving early
- social withdrawal and taking frustration out on others
- using food, drugs, or alcohol to cope
- problems sleeping and loss of sex drive.

Stress as the new normal

The problem with contemporary society is that stress tends to creep up on us. The world around us is not quite what nature intended. We were designed to roam in fields and pick fruit off trees; however, our children often learn to use technology before they can walk and talk. Even though technological advancements are incredible and allow us to live an existence of ease compared to our ancestors, in today's technologically driven world our body is not getting the down time it needs and we end up existing in a state of heightened stress a large amount of the time. It's like we've become used to stress as our new normal. We don't notice the extent to which stress is affecting us even as it takes a heavy toll. This level of chronic stress is a contributing factor to the anxiety epidemic we're experiencing. Anxiety rates are on the rise as our body and brain get bombarded by the impact of 'always being on'.

Alongside the feelings of overwhelm that technology can breed comes an erosion of the kind of connection we need – we need eye contact, we need human touch.

Human beings are tribal beings. There is safety in the tribe and safety in connection. Tribal members who were outliers were at risk of being attacked by a predator. Staying close to the members of their tribe meant that they were protected. So, we crave connection; we are comforted and nurtured by it. The neurochemical reaction is a surge of oxytocin – the neurochemical for attachment, for cohesion – in the bloodstream. This instils a sense of calm and contentment.

However, instead we are addicted to our mobile phone and find it hard to let go. So we don't look up at each other, we don't look at our friends, we don't look at our kids and they don't look at us. This has critical implications for how we evolve as individuals and as a society as a whole. The early development of emotional intelligence becomes undermined. It is now commonplace for toddlers to be handed a mobile phone or a tablet. As loving parents, we do it because we want to offer the educational tools that are easily accessible for our little ones – we feel the need in order to keep up. Similarly, connection becomes eroded at school and in the workplace. We send an email to a work colleague rather than walk a few metres to where they are seated. It is hard to not get sucked into the vortex of digital technology. Ultimately, however, digital technology is an illusion of connection – in essence, it's disconnection.

The result of these combined factors is that in our complex society, worry is rampant and there is an epidemic of stress and anxiety. We have reached a tipping point, where the technological saturation is overwhelming our capacity to cope. This is being evidenced in the rates of clinical anxiety, depression, stress, self-harm and suicide.

However, the good news is that it is remediable through the evidence-based strategies of the Mind Strength Method. Step 3 gives you a toolkit to build resilience and Step 4 provides a Mind Strength Wellbeing Pyramid and an action plan to bolster your mind and body against burnout.

———

You also want to change your relationship with your emotions. All too readily, society delivers the message that feelings mean that you are weak, that you are no good and that you need to stifle your emotions and shut them down. This is the concept of distress intolerance, which I believe is wreaking havoc on our society. In the next chapter, we'll look into this concept in detail – and the alternative approach that is central to the Mind Strength Method: distress tolerance.

Chapter 9

Distress tolerance

It's not about not having uncomfortable feelings,
it's how we respond to the feelings that matters

At the heart of the Mind Strength Method is the concept of distress tolerance. Distress tolerance says that all feelings are okay: emotions are a natural and normal part of being human. It is not about *not* having big feelings, but about responding to your feelings with helpful rather than unhelpful actions. This runs counter to the social stigma associated with the experience of big emotions and our tendency to think we need to shut them down for fear of not being seen as 'good enough'. This is called distress intolerance, which leads to an intensification of stress, burnout and serious mental health challenges, such as self-harm and suicide.

A prolonged state of stress can lead to an experience of distress. When you are in a state of distress, it can lead to mental health challenges such as depression and anxiety. Worry thoughts can start to take hold and, before you know it, you are caught in a vortex of large and challenging emotions. This is when society chimes in and says, 'You can't be experiencing

big emotions! That means that you're not coping – that means you're not good enough.' Social media kicks you while you are down, as everyone is presenting their airbrushed, perfect versions of themselves, which only intensifies your experience of not feeling good enough. This problem of 'compare and despair' reinforces the tendency to want to hide big emotions. This is a tough and unrealistic expectation. This is distress intolerance.

Distress intolerance says feelings are weak, feelings are bad, feelings are a failure and you must therefore block them, avoid them and shut them down.

However, the attempt to block big emotions has the opposite effect of its intended purpose, as it results in a loss of emotional control. Distress intolerance typically leads to a Mount Vesuvius of emotions – a high intensity of emotions rather than none at all.

As you begin to recognise that emotions can't just be 'shut down', you turn to ways to 'numb' big emotions. Examples include unhelpful coping strategies such as drugs, alcohol, gaming, sex, porn, comfort-eating, self-harm, and the ultimate attempt to numb difficult emotions, suicide.

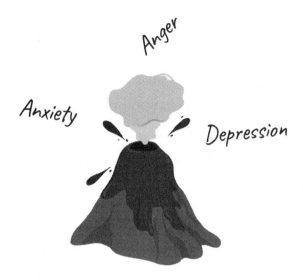

Distress intolerance results in us getting hooked into a vicious cycle. Distress leads to compulsive and addictive behaviours to wipe out the stress. However, these quick fixes in the short term end up increasing stress in the long term. Distress intolerance keeps you trapped in the fight or flight pathway and moves you away from values-driven actions that provide a sense of meaning, purpose and fulfilment. Distress intolerance prevents us from learning transformational strategies to alleviate distress and realign with values. Instead, we numb distress and remain trapped.

Although distress intolerance impacts both men and women, the message of 'it's weak to feel' is particularly prevalent among men who are told from a young age to 'man up' and that 'boys don't cry'.

Mike was caught in a spiral of distress intolerance. He had turned to alcohol as a way of coping with the challenging emotions of anxiety, anger, agitation and low mood. The problem was that alcohol was a clear 'flight' behaviour, an attempt to numb his emotions and avoid the challenges he needed to face. Alcohol was leading to further withdrawal from his family and emotional outbursts that were way out of alignment with his and his family's values. It led to deep and destructive emotions of guilt and shame that his children and his wife were witness to this emotional decline.

Adam experienced stress and anxiety brought about by a fear of not being able to get his schoolwork done effectively. As a result, he retreated inwards. He withdrew from family; he withdrew from friends. He spent hours in his bedroom and found a reprieve from big emotions through the numbing experiences of gaming addiction. However, shutting down the emotions was an illusion of control. The byproduct of this was an increase in more explosive emotions in his interactions with his parents. Adam eventually learned to recognise that all his feelings were okay – that it was not about not having the feelings but about how he responded to them that mattered.

● ● ●

Mike and Adam's challenges are all too common in our society. Social conventions and social media increasingly place pressure on us to be perfect in every facet of our lives. The belief that we need to be all-coping is drummed into us from an early age. An external facade of stoicism and strength belies our inherent human vulnerabilities. Having difficult feelings is a normal and shared human experience. Anxiety, sadness, fear, anger, frustration and embarrassment are common to us all. It is how we respond to these feelings that matters.

Building mind strength is a fundamental shift from distress intolerance. The Mind Strength Toolkit equips you with a number of helpful actions in response to big emotions. It shows you the alternative pathway to distress tolerance – observing, accepting and allowing emotions, and responding with kindness, compassion, self-awareness and resilience.

———

Look at what you've learned! You've built awareness of the fight or flight reaction. You understand what anxiety, stress and fear are, and why these functions play an incredibly important role when we need them. You also recognise that you don't want to shut down big feelings. Instead, you want to observe and understand these feelings, both the physiological and emotional experiences of anxiety.

Alongside understanding the fight or flight driven feelings, Step 1 of the Mind Strength Method is about understanding fight or flight driven thoughts and actions. The main driver of these thoughts is worry. Now, it's time to turn our attention to the bully in our minds and explore worry in closer detail.

Chapter 10

The worry snowball

Worry is your brain's attempt to
predict your environment in order
to achieve certainty and control

When you worry, your brain is responding to a perceived threat as if it were a real threat: a tiger in your midst ready to pounce. It interprets the worry thought ('I'm going to fail!') as if it were a real danger ('That tiger is going to kill me!'), triggering a surge of adrenaline and cortisol through your bloodstream, which you experience as anxiety. Sometimes the worry thoughts are niggling doubts that play quietly in the background, and at other times worry is like a foghorn, a nasty bully inside your head. Worry's close cousin is rumination, a focus on something negative that might have happened in the past. You fear that you have done something stupid, so you dwell on the situation and circumstances to try to make sense of it.

We typically engage in worry and rumination because we think they are serving a helpful purpose: focusing on all the possible things that might go wrong or might have gone wrong means that you won't miss anything, right? You engage in the 'what ifs' and the 'should haves' because you're keen to get things right, to do the right thing by others, to protect yourself and to protect the people you care about.

Worry and rumination are both part of your primitive survival mechanism to be able to predict your environment. In an uncertain situation, you engage in these mental processes to try to feel more in control. The problem is that both worry and rumination have the opposite effect to their intended purpose – instead of helping you to feel more in control, they just lead you to focus on all the bad things that might happen or might have happened, so you end up feeling more out of control. Instead of feeling more certain, you end up feeling more uncertain. So worry and rumination actually make you feel worse rather than better. They are not a weakness; they are just part of being human. But they can, at times, feel like an inner bully bossing you around – and, like any real-life bully, the more attention you give to worry or rumination, the more powerful they become.

Recall also that these types of mental processes typically tend to boss around the people who care just that little bit more – people who are perhaps kinder, or have a more analytical mind. I call it a Ferrari mind, a deep-thinking mind that can want to rev up its engine from time to time. Like a Ferrari, it requires just a little maintenance and fine-tuning to be able to embrace its full awesomeness – and when it does it's brilliant. So what you want to do is celebrate that analytical mind and empathic heart and learn to stand up to the challenges.

Mike's main worries were about his finances.
He spent a lot of his time worrying that he
wouldn't have enough money to fund his family's
future needs. He second-guessed himself about
investments he had made and questioned whether he had done the
right thing. He worried to the point of catastrophising, focusing on
all of the things that might go wrong with his investments. Mike's
fear of making the wrong decision often resulted in him making no
decisions. He commonly stayed trapped in inertia due to fear of
failure. He regularly checked and rechecked the stock market and
sought reassurance from those around him.

Like Mike, Ella worried about making a mistake, specifically in
relation to her work. Ella's worries revolved predominantly around
letting people down, or not being seen to be good enough. She also
worried about the wellbeing of her children. Worry was particularly
bullish at night when she was trying to sleep. Typically, she
struggled with her worry thoughts, tried to push them out of her
mind or tried to convince herself that she had nothing to worry
about. The problem was that not only were these strategies
unhelpful, they actually made her feel worse rather than better
– worry set in more strongly.

Worry and rumination were big bullies in Allie's life, too.
She feared saying something incorrect or embarrassing herself in
class, despite having worked incredibly hard. She knew the answers
but self-doubt crept in and got the better of her. She failed to speak
up and second-guessed herself in social situations for fear of
being judged negatively. She went over past events in her mind
repeatedly to make sure that she hadn't humiliated herself or
done the wrong thing by anyone.

Adam worried about failing his exams. He found it hard to focus when trying to study, as worry whispered that he would stuff up and not be good enough. He found it hard to get to sleep at night because he was focusing on all the things that might go wrong. The more he worried, the more anxious he felt and the more he feared he wouldn't be good enough. Worry was clearly wreaking havoc not just on Adam but also on his relationship with his family, who loved him dearly. The best way Adam found to shut down the voice of worry was to numb his mind with social media and computer games, which took on addictive elements of their own.

Luke had a specific worry that dogs were dangerous and would attack him if he encountered one. He would think about the possibility of coming into contact with a dog in order to prepare for the worst. He picked up on news stories about dog attacks to listen out for the circumstances in which they happened, in order to make sure that he avoided those circumstances. He found himself thinking about dogs a lot and felt pretty miserable seeing his friends having fun at parties, parks and sleepovers. His parents were increasingly concerned about the impact these worry thoughts were having on Luke's life and his subsequent avoidance of sporting and social events.

● ● ●

In order to catch your attention, it is not enough for worry to just say that something bad will happen. Worry alerts you to the possibility that it will be an absolute disaster, a catastrophe, and that you won't have the skills, the capacity or the resilience to cope. It keeps you primed towards self-protection – that's its job. But you can beat it.

THE WORRY BULLY

Worry is antsy: it will scream and shout in order to catch your attention. Worry also has a phenomenal imagination. It will conjure up images and scripts about all the possible things that might go wrong. In fact, it is an epic fiction writer – an award-winning novelist – and the star of the story is you, your family, your loved ones, your friends, your finances, your health, everything in your life that you want to keep safe, protected and well.

However, it is an illusion of safety. In fact, worry works counter to your values. It moves you away from what gives you a sense of wellbeing. In order to trick you into thinking that it is keeping you and your loved ones safe, protected and well, it tells you to avoid, avoid, avoid. It tells you to move right away from all the things that are important to you.

Worry tells you to struggle and fight to get certainty and control. It tells you that you have to be perfect in order to be okay and you have to please everyone in order to be good enough. It says do everything for everyone because otherwise people might, in fact, discover that you are an imposter and a fraud. It is the sneakiest con artist there is.

And sometimes worry tells you to attack in order to protect yourself, and to lash out at others because otherwise they will see your vulnerabilities and your flaws. You'd better defend yourself because otherwise a catastrophe might happen. Check, plan, prepare, over-control and never, ever delegate, in order to make sure that you and all you care about will be okay.

Worry must know the future. It must have absolute certainty and it must protect. Worry and rumination then enlist their posse, the critical voice and depression, who pipe up to say shut down and withdraw, because you're just not worth it, you'll never be worth it and nobody cares anyway.

In essence, worry and rumination are illusions of control and protection – they just get you focused on the negatives. Think of them like a snowball rolling down a mountain gathering more snow ... it just gets bigger and bigger! So worry just ends up leading to ... that's right ... more worry.

The benefit of this conceptualisation is that you can begin to recognise both worry and rumination as futile mental processes. It is not so much about getting caught up in the

content of the thoughts, but rather starting to notice what kind of thought it is and considering whether it is a helpful or an unhelpful kind of thought. Rather than getting hooked into the content, you can start to loosen your belief that worry and rumination actually help you. It is a large step on the path to bossing worry and rumination back and not letting them have the same power over you as they had before.

———

The good news is that there are practical, simple and effective alternatives to worry and rumination. In Part 3 of the Mind Strength Method, I will run through the Mind Strength Toolkit to show you what these are. You will learn how to stand up to worry and rumination, and get some distance from these mental actions so they don't take control. I will show you how to change your relationship with worry, realign with your values, engage in the things that are important to you, and live an empowered, fulfilled life.

Chapter 11

Building self-awareness

We can only change what we are
aware of in the first place

Self-awareness is key to building mental strength and resilience. You want to notice and label when worry or rumination are bossing you around. Awareness of your fear-driven thoughts and actions is a critical first step in overcoming stress and anxiety. Start by noticing the voice of worry. See if you can begin to think about worry like a bully bossing you around. Consider it a pesky rascal trying to hassle you to make up for its own insecurities. You now know that worry serves no purpose. By acknowledging this, you can far more readily loosen the shackles binding it to you. You can now change your relationship with worry and reconceptualise it as a futile mental process.

A powerful tool in your Mind Strength Toolkit (as you will see in Step 3 of the Mind Strength Method) is to start to think about worry telling you a tedious and boring story and conceptualising the worry thoughts as a book.

Some common themes for worry stories are

- fear of loss of control
- fear of failure
- fear of change
- fear of disapproval
- fear of being assertive
- fear of making a decision
- fear of making a mistake
- fear of rejection
- fear of embarrassing yourself
- fear of public speaking
- fear of a physical health problem
- fear of harm
- fear of uncertainty.

Do any of these stories ring true for you? Remember, if you are experiencing worries such as these, you are definitely not alone. Whether you're at work, with your family, at a restaurant, at a party, at a presentation, or in any other number of situations, when you look around you, approximately one in every four adults, children and adolescents will be experiencing some form of worry thoughts that escalate into more severe anxiety.

Worry can make you not go to the event you'd love to go to, or not speak to the people you'd love to speak to, or not do the work that you know you need to do because you just think you're not going to be any good at it. It can make you lose belief in yourself and feel stressed out and awful. As with any bully, when you pay attention to the worry thoughts, they get bigger, more threatening and harder to ignore – just like the snowball on page 88.

Typically, the challenge is not actually a 'mistakes are a disaster' problem or a 'people won't like me' problem or a 'dog' problem or an 'I might get very sick' problem – the challenge is

a 'worry' problem. In essence, our human predisposition is to struggle with uncertainty, and the good news is you always have a choice about whether to listen to worry or not. When you recognise worry as a futile mental process that actually makes you feel worse rather than better, it becomes much easier to release yourself from the shackles of worry.

You can choose to listen to the worry thoughts and let worry tell you what to do or not to do. When you choose to listen to worry and let worry boss you around then worry gets stronger and more powerful. Alternatively, you can take a different approach by following these four steps.

1. Notice when worry is bossing you around.
2. Label it as worry.
3. Use the tools in your toolkit to stand up to worry and BOSS WORRY BACK.
4. Move on with heart-driven, practical action.

So, now that you have reflected on your fight or flight driven feelings and your fight or flight driven thoughts, it's time to shift focus to your fight or flight driven actions. What are some of the amygdala-driven behaviours that typically take hold when you are perceiving a threat in your environment?

The amygdala is like a rambunctious little puppy and likes to assert itself. Nature has designed you that way in order to keep you alive in the case of a real threat. The amygdala is pre-programmed to take you towards fight or fight behaviours. Let's now explore what that rambunctious little amygdala puppy tells you to do.

Get to know your worry thoughts

Think about the last time you felt stressed, anxious or agitated.

- What was the situation?
- What thoughts were playing out in your mind? Was there some future unknown or previous action that you were concerned about? What were worry or rumination tricking you into thinking and believing? What was the worry story? Did the thoughts increase their power over you when you listened to them?
- How did you feel when you listened to what worry and rumination had to say? Did you get stressed out? Did the anxiety get worse?

Spend a few days noting down the kinds of worry or rumination thoughts that come up. Get to know what worry and rumination sound like and the ways they try to hook you into dwelling on perceived negatives from the past or convince you about bad things happening in the future.

Notice when the worry thoughts are trying to boss you around. Recognise the sound of worry's voice and the tricks it tries to play – what is it telling you? Remember that worry can be very convincing. A bully will try to provoke you. But, as you know, a bully is often only a bully if you give it attention. Get a bit of distance from your thoughts. Be an objective observer. Remember you always have a choice of whether to listen to worry or to stand up to it and not give it the attention it's demanding.

Chapter 12

Safety behaviours

Unhelpful coping strategies that
undermine your capacity for resilience

When you go down the fear and worry pathway, your protector, the amygdala, takes over and gets you to engage in all sorts of fight or flight driven mental and physical actions. These actions might be helpful, and downright essential, in times of real danger, but they are unhelpful in response to worry thoughts. When you respond to a perceived threat as if it is real, the behaviours that you engage in are called 'safety behaviours' or unhelpful coping strategies.

Safety behaviours are adopted with the intention of pushing away from fear and worry, rather than with the intention of pulling towards a life aligned with your values. They prevent you from building resilience – you don't allow yourself to sit with the discomfort of uncertainty or to sit with the discomfort of imperfection and learn that you can cope. They keep you locked in your cosy little comfort zone with your nice fluffy slippers where it's all very safe and predictable.

The problem is you don't end up living your life in alignment with what's important to you – a life of heart-driven action. These unhelpful coping strategies can wreak havoc in your career, in your relationships and in your capacity to live your life. Not only are these behaviours unhelpful but they keep you trapped in your fears and typically make your anxiety worse rather than better.

A good way to understand safety behaviours is to think of them like 'struggling in quicksand'. Typically, you struggle because you think that it is helping you to escape from the threatening situation. But what actually happens when you struggle in quicksand? That's right: you sink in deeper. You end up in a worse situation rather than better.

Just like struggling in quicksand, fight or flight driven actions in response to a perceived threat, rather than a real threat, get in the way of you living your life effectively. They prevent you from learning that nothing bad was actually going to happen, or that, even if things didn't go exactly according to plan, it wasn't a catastrophe and you coped.

Avoid, escape
Procrastinate, take a sickie, numb the feelings through binge drinking, comfort eating, self-harm, suicide

Get certainty and control
Over-check, over-control, fail to delegate, seek reassurance, try to be perfect

Attack, defend
Finger-point, blame, triangulate, gossip, undermine others, be aggressive

The challenge is that, typically, we don't allow ourselves to demonstrate that worry was wrong, and instead we think that we were only okay because of the safety behaviours.

Safety behaviours can be both mental and physical actions and tend to cluster around three core areas:

1. The 'fight'
2. The 'flight'
3. Things to achieve 'certainty and control'.

'Fight' safety behaviours

Attack, defend, finger-point, blame

These safety behaviours cluster around the 'fight' in the fight or flight reaction. Anger, agitation and frustration are representations of the hijacking amygdala – and part of our physiological reaction to perceived threat. Behavioural representations might be overt acts of aggression, such as attacking others or being defensive, or they may be more subtle representations, such as finger-pointing, blaming, bullying or gossiping.

These emotions and associated behavioural representations can be manifestations of masked anxiety. These faces of anxiety are not commonly known and can be misinterpreted as aggressive, resulting inadvertently in incorrect labels and inappropriate strategies to remedy these emotions. This is particularly true among children and adolescents, who may be incorrectly labelled as 'oppositional', 'hyperactive' or 'inattentive' when, in fact, they are experiencing anxiety. When we help the anxiety, the challenging behaviours dissolve.

At times, people who attempt to push their emotions down through flight behaviours can oscillate back towards fight behaviours. These safety behaviours undermine the potential for effective relationships and are also often out of alignment with a person's values. Think of Mike: anxiety and stress tipped him into anger and aggression, and he found himself lashing out at his wife and children. These undesired behaviours led to other challenging emotions of guilt and shame, further intensifying Mike's distress and keeping him trapped in a vicious cycle of self-destruction.

'Flight' safety behaviours

Avoidance

The primary unhelpful coping strategy that we commonly engage in when going down the flight pathway is avoidance. We listen to the voice of worry and, as a result, avoid the bad things that worry is telling us will happen. For example, if worry is telling you that dogs will bite you, you stay away from places where you might see dogs. Alternatively, if worry is telling you that you will mess up your presentation, you might make up an excuse for not presenting and arrange for somebody else to do it instead.

Escape

Alternatively, you might already be in a specific situation and worry is telling you to escape. Commonly, what we want to escape from is not the situation itself but rather the sensations of the fight or flight reaction while we are in that situation. We feel the fear and anxiety and perceive it as a potential catastrophe, so we leave the situation. Recall the panic spiral. When you escape the situation, you no longer experience the physiological sensations of the fight or flight reaction, which in turn reinforces the escape behaviours. You begin to perceive the situation as the source of the danger and associate escape from that situation as safety. You never allow yourself to learn that nothing bad was going to happen in that situation or that the problem was, in fact, your fear of something bad happening and the sensations associated with that fear, rather than the situation itself.

Passivity and people-pleasing

Other safety behaviours on the 'flight' path are being passive or submissive. These include not standing up for yourself, apologising unnecessarily, or engaging in people-pleasing actions for the sole purpose of avoiding the possibility of someone judging you negatively.

To determine whether or not these behaviours are safety behaviours, ask yourself whether they are driven by fear or driven by values. For example, abundant acts of kindness are to be embraced and treasured if they are values-driven. However, if they are done for the sole purpose of preventing someone from judging you negatively and worry is telling you that unless you please everyone something bad is going to happen, then they become safety behaviours and unhelpful coping strategies.

Procrastination

Another common safety behaviour on the flight path is procrastination. You know what you have to do, you know how to do it, you very much want to do it, but you just can't seem to stop yourself from procrastinating. If you have experienced this, you know how tough it can be. It is like a big, brick wall between you and the tasks that you very much want and need to achieve.

Procrastination is another way that your amygdala is trying to protect you by getting you to run away when you don't need it to, and you don't want it to. It is a strong and stubborn safety behaviour driven by fear of a threatening outcome. Commonly, that threatening outcome is making a mistake, failing, or being seen to be 'not good enough'. It is often caused by perfectionism, where the underlying belief is 'I have to be

perfect in order to be good enough'. The Mind Strength Method has helped thousands of people to break down that brick wall of procrastination – and it will help you too.

Blocking your thoughts

Other safety behaviours are the mental actions you try to perform in order to block your negative or worry thoughts. Like most safety behaviours, these are counterintuitive. Logic might tell you that if you have an intrusive negative thought or worry thought you should try to block and somehow get rid of it; after all, you don't want the worry thoughts to be there – you'd rather they just go away. This is the way we are programmed as humans: if we have something aversive or unpleasant in our experiences, we try to get rid of it. So you begin to struggle with your worry thoughts. You try to push them out of your mind, to get rid of them and block them. And does this work? Nuh-uh. Your mind just wants to think.

This is what minds do. When you try to push your thoughts out of your mind, they become louder, stronger and more front of mind. To see this in action, take a moment to try the 'pink elephant' experiment below.

MIND STRENGTH ACTION

Don't think of the pink elephant!

If you have a mobile phone with you or an alarm on your watch, set your timer for 30 seconds. Now, for the next 30 seconds until the timer goes off, whatever you do, do not think of a pink elephant. Ready? Okay ... go.

What was the outcome? It's pretty impossible, huh? And not only is it impossible but it has the opposite effect of its intended purpose – all of a sudden, you start seeing the pink elephant more obviously, or the pink elephant's friends decide to join in.

This is the effect of trying to block your worry thoughts – it is a futile mental process. Not only that, but it actually ends up exacerbating your worry thoughts and they become front and centre in your mind.

Distraction

Distraction is a subtle safety behaviour similar to blocking your thoughts. If you distract yourself from your thoughts, it might help you in the short term, but they have a habit of bouncing right back in. For this reason, distraction with the intention of avoiding and blocking negative or worry thoughts is typically unhelpful. Keep in mind that this is different from the distraction that occurs as a result of pivoting and adjusting away from your worry thoughts and realigning with values-driven goals and actions. One is the push away from worry and the other is the pull towards a desired direction. One is going down the fight or flight path and the other is alignment with values. Ask yourself if your action is fear-driven (unhelpful safety behaviour) or values-driven (helpful heart-driven action) and pivot towards values.

Numbing emotions through self-destructive behaviours

Another cluster of 'flight' safety behaviours are attempts to numb big emotions due to distress intolerance. Distress intolerance is brought about by cultural messages of stigma and shame associated with experiencing big emotions. If you have a challenging emotion such as anger, fear, embarrassment, frustration or sadness, you might feel like the only way you will cope is if you engage in strategies to numb these feelings. This can lead to a vicious cycle of self-destructive behaviours, which in turn increases stress levels, anxiety and agitation. This can lead again to unhelpful safety behaviours to further numb the big emotions. Some examples of these types of self-destructive behaviours include

* recreational drug and alcohol consumption
* gambling
* gaming
* indiscriminate sexual behaviours

- binge eating
- self-harm
- the ultimate unhelpful coping strategy in an attempt to numb big emotions: suicide.

Let's explore some of the unhelpful mental and physical coping strategies that kept Mike, Ella, Allie and Adam trapped in their fears. In Mike's case, the most prevalent mental safety behaviours were worry, rumination and second-guessing himself. Some behavioural coping strategies included checking and rechecking his financial management strategy, repeatedly seeking reassurance from his wife and financial advisers, checking the internet for any health symptoms, scanning his body for symptoms, getting repeat check-ups from his doctor and specialists, and turning to alcohol to numb his stress and anxiety. Mike found that some of these checking behaviours would make him feel better momentarily but then the doubt would creep in again and he was as agitated and stressed as ever. What's more, the more he checked the internet, the more he read about things happening to other people, which would escalate his worry and anxiety even further. He became hypervigilant, wondering whether something even more sinister was going on.

Alongside worry and checking behaviours, Ella's primary safety behaviour was perfectionism. Her belief was that she had to be perfect in order to be okay. Perfectionism gave her a false sense of comfort because being perfect meant there would be no uncertainty about how others judged her and nothing bad would happen. Fear of not being good enough in the eyes of her colleagues, friends and family led Ella to withdraw socially. As social withdrawal was out of alignment with her values, her mood started to go down, which led to more social withdrawal, thereby triggering an unhelpful and damaging downward spiral, tipping Ella towards depression.

Allie also had many fear-driven mental safety behaviours, including worry, rumination and mind reading, as well as physical safety behaviours including checking how she looked, browsing social media, comparing herself to others and seeking reassurance. She avoided speaking up in her university tutorials and avoided going out. Like Ella, she felt that she was only okay if she was perfect, which kept her stuck in a permanent mental state of 'I'm not good enough'.

Safety behaviours were also keeping Adam trapped in a vicious spiral of anxiety, distress and suffering. He worried about not being good enough at his schoolwork and not being able to get his assignments done effectively, so he avoided studying and procrastinated extensively. His other avoidance strategies included using social media and computer games. He also lashed out at his family – a fight safety behaviour – and shut himself away.

Luke's primary safety behaviour was avoidance. He begged his parents not to make him go to parks, friends' houses or parties where a dog might be present. In maintaining this strict avoidance, Luke prevented himself from learning that nothing bad was going to happen. He also sought reassurance from his parents, and they would often give him reassurance in advance of certain situations to prevent a meltdown.

'Certainty and control' safety behaviours

As we know, human beings do not sit comfortably with uncertainty. We struggle with it. It taps in to our biological survival instinct, which says that if we leave our cave and can't see around the corner a predator might be there ready to gobble us up. There are many safety behaviours specifically for the purpose of eliminating uncertainty and achieving control.

Worry

The primary safety behaviour in an attempt to gain certainty and control is worry. The problem with worry is you focus on all the possible things that might go wrong so you end up feeling worse rather than better. It digs you deeper into your fear rather than lifting you out of it. A negative outcome is the inevitable path of worry – by the very nature of worry it is not a story with a happy ending. Worry in its extreme form is called catastrophising. This is where the snowball leads you to dwell on the worst-case scenario.

Ruminate

Akin to worry is rumination. Again, the purpose of rumination is to try to work out your past experiences to feel more certain and in control, but it just ends up making you feel more uncertain and more out of control. This unhelpful coping strategy is a struggle of the darkest kind, where the critical voice is rampant about an individual's perceived 'not good enoughs' and 'shouldn't haves'.

Mind reading

Mind reading, another destructive safety behaviour relating to certainty and control, is the attempt to work out what someone else is thinking about you. The problem with mind reading is that you will never truly know what somebody else is thinking, so you will always be struggling with uncertainty. And as we now know, this struggle with uncertainty triggers the hijacking amygdala and the fight or flight reaction. In other words, anxiety!

Combine mind reading with the human brain's inherent negativity bias and it's not a great outcome. Keeping in mind that you will never know what somebody else is thinking about you, in the absence of clear-cut evidence, the negativity bias means you are far more likely to think that they are thinking all sorts of negative 'not good enoughs' about you rather than something positive or neutral. If your worry story is fear of being judged negatively, hypervigilance to threat will play even greater tricks on you. So you mind read to try to feel more in control but you end up focusing on all the possible negative things that the other person could be thinking about you – and you end up feeling more out of control. As you can only change what you are aware of in the first place, awareness of when your mind is engaging in mind reading is powerful. As with worry, you can notice the unhelpful mental process of mind reading, label it as 'mind reading' and get some distance from it rather than getting caught up.

Challenging, arguing, rationalising

These mental gymnastics are similar to blocking your thoughts or distraction (see pages 103–105). This is your attempt to get rid of the worry thoughts through logic. Logic is telling you that if you have an intrusive negative thought or worry thought, you should struggle with its content. However, anxiety does not play out in logical ways, and your attempts to appeal to the worry thoughts typically makes things worse – you inadvertently dig yourself in deeper. Once again, when you argue with your worry thoughts and try to get rid of the worry, it is like you are in the boxing ring, having a fight with uncertainty. You are engaging in these mental safety behaviours because you think it's helping you to get more certainty and control, but what generally happens is you end up feeling more uncertain, more out of control and more anxious.

Over-checking and reassurance seeking

Other attempts to achieve certainty and control are checking behaviours and reassurance seeking. You might check and recheck your work or check your body and your environment, or you might seek reassurance from your family, friends or business colleagues. The challenge is that the checking responses and reassurance seeking will help momentarily but then the doubt creeps back in, because, in essence, you're seeking certainty when there is no certainty – you're seeking a futile outcome. Not only does the doubt creep back in, but the action of being provided with reassurance in the moment reduces your stress and anxiety, which is enough to motivate you to check or seek reassurance again. However, the doubt creeps back in again, so you are sent into a perpetual cycle that looks like this.

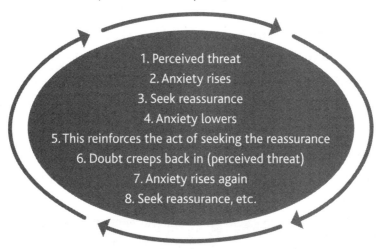

Help! You are trapped in safety behaviour quicksand and you spiral down!

1. Perceived threat
2. Anxiety rises
3. Seek reassurance
4. Anxiety lowers
5. This reinforces the act of seeking the reassurance
6. Doubt creeps back in (perceived threat)
7. Anxiety rises again
8. Seek reassurance, etc.

Perfectionism

Perfectionism is the quintessential fear-driven safety behaviour in the pursuit of certainty and control. You strive for perfection to prevent something bad from happening. You know that if it is perfect, then there is no possibility of being judged negatively. The problem, however, is that the pursuit of perfection results in unachievable or unsustainable standards, and individuals who strive to be perfect in order to feel good enough never end up feeling good enough. As a result, perfectionism undermines self-esteem and self-perception, and leaves you in a permanent state of stress. You are trapped in fight or flight, and what are you fighting? The fear of imperfection. Moreover, hypervigilance to threat means that if you focus in on what you feel threatened by and your threat is fear of not being good enough, your brain is going to tip towards all of your perceived 'not good enoughs' – so the pursuit of perfection is a no-win objective. It is a fear-driven safety behaviour where the only direction is spiralling down.

Over-preparing

Over-preparing, over-arranging and over-cleaning are also behaviours representative of the pursuit of certainty and control. But, as with distraction (see pages 104–105), it is important to reflect on what is driving these behaviours. If they are fear-driven – a fear of failure, being judged negatively or making a mistake, for example – this would imply that they are unhelpful coping strategies. If, however, these behaviours are values-driven, these are the actions to be embraced (see below for more about this).

MIND STRENGTH ACTION

Look out for safety behaviours

Consider what fight or flight driven actions you perform to cope in the short term. Think about the last few times you felt anxious, agitated or stressed. What were the situations? What was worry telling you to do in those situations? Can you write down the mental or physical behaviours you engaged in. Safety behaviours can be subtle, so look out for them.

Notice, label and let go

Self-awareness is pivotal in determining whether a mental or physical action is helpful or unhelpful. If your action is fear-driven in response to a worry thought, then it is more than likely going to be a safety behaviour. The road ahead is about building clarity and awareness of those safety behaviours.

These are the steps to follow:

1. Notice the unhelpful mental or physical process.
2. Label the safety behaviour.
3. Let go of the fight or flight driven response and re-engage in a helpful values-driven alternative.

This is a powerful strategy to bring you another step closer to turning anxiety into effective action and worry into wellbeing!

The good news is that for people who experience anxiety, anticipation is often so much worse than the reality. The problem is that worry can be very convincing and, when you listen to worry, you don't allow yourself to move beyond anticipation – you don't end up facing your fears or letting go of your safety behaviours. You stay in that cosy comfort zone with your warm fluffy slippers and cup of tea, but you never take the steps to living your best life.

As you can see, these safety behaviours only push you deeper into your worries. You avoid rather than approach. By listening to worry and doing what worry tells you, you prevent yourself from

- developing the skills you need
- learning that bad things would not have happened
- learning that you would have coped a lot better than it tricked you into believing you would.

It is only when you let go of these behaviours and approach avoided situations that you learn you would have been okay. In reality, bad things are generally far less likely to happen than worry would have you think; the outcome is generally not nearly as awful as worry leads you to believe; and you generally cope a lot better than worry is telling you. When you listen to worry, you end up feeling a lot worse than you need to feel! So, take a moment to think about what worry is tricking you into believing, remember that thoughts are just thoughts and see if you can start to get a bit of distance from them.

Accepting uncertainty

As you now know, the overarching problem is that you are struggling to gain certainty when there is no certainty – you will never be able to know definitively. This struggle with uncertainty keeps you trapped in anxiety; it keeps the amygdala firing because you are in fight or flight mode. But here's the catch. You're not fighting a fear of dogs, or a fear of being judged negatively, or a fear of something bad happening to a loved one – you're fighting uncertainty. While you continue to struggle with uncertainty rather than accept it as an inevitable part of life, you are going to keep your brain's car alarm firing and keep yourself feeling anxious.

So what's the alternative? The alternative to grappling or fighting with uncertainty is acceptance or tolerance of uncertainty. This is no easy task. Your brain is wired to seek certainty in order to keep you safe. But while it might be challenging to sit with the discomfort of uncertainty, it is doable! In finding freedom from anxiety, you need to allow yourself to learn that even if things don't go completely according to plan, you build up a capacity to cope. By moving through anxiety rather than avoiding it, you develop the courage and confidence to face a life aligned with your values rather than dictated by fear.

Soon we'll go through a whole toolkit of mind strength strategies to help you in that challenge. The Mind Strength Toolkit will help you to move from anxiety to effective action, build resilience and find freedom from fear. Using and revisiting the strategies in this book will help you to change your relationship with the problem, feel more empowered to stand up to worry and live your best life.

Before you become an expert in the tools to build mind strength, it's time to build clarity around the alternative pathway to fear, worry, anger, aggression and depression. That alternative pathway aligns with your heart – it is the pull towards your desired direction in life. This is the roadmap of your purpose and values.

Step 1 Summary

Great work moving through Step 1! You are now able to

1. understand anxiety and associated physiological and emotional reactions
2. identify your worry thoughts
3. name your worry story
4. recognise your unhelpful safety behaviours
5. see the benefits in facing your worry story and sitting with the discomfort of uncertainty.

Now you are ready to move on to Step 2.

STEP

2

Awareness
of your values

Chapter 13

The alternative to fear-driven actions

Values-driven actions are the pull towards meaning rather than the push away from fear

You're now well positioned to notice when worry is bossing you around. You recognise that the fear-driven pathway often takes you to a destination filled with even greater uncertainty and anxiety. You recognise that you need to stand up to worry by not engaging in safety behaviours. But this is hard. Worry can be very convincing, and when we've got the hijacking amygdala on speed dial, our capacity for rational judgement is clouded.

The Mind Strength Toolkit will make it easier to stand up to the hijacking amygdala. But in order to be able to pivot away from the fight or flight pathway, you need an alternative road to go down. Rather than living your life being pushed away from worry and fear, you want to live your life being pulled towards ... something. The question is, what is that something? How do you know which thoughts to listen to and which ones to stand up to? The answer comes from your heart.

Guided by values

Values are like the foundations of a magnificent architectural structure – and that architectural structure is you. A strong building is built on solid foundations, which enable the building to stay stable, even in the most turbulent weather. You, too, will feel more stable if you are built on solid foundations, in this case, your values. Alignment with your values will bolster your resilience against anxiety, low mood and stress, and will lead to a greater sense of fulfilment and wellness.

Your values are the things that are deeply important to you. They are your guiding directions in life. Some examples of values are kindness, courage, creativity, authenticity, loyalty and fun. There is no judgement around values. Everybody values different sorts of things, and it's up to you to reflect on what's important to you.

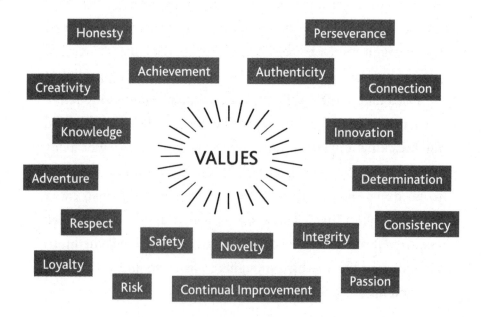

Typically, we have limited clarity when it comes to our own values. We are fairly quick to identify our 'push away from' fear-driven actions, but find it hard to clarify our 'pull towards' things that we value. Why is this the case? Why do we find it easy to identify the things we don't want from life, but find it tricky to achieve clarity on our values and the things that are the most important to us? Again, it goes back to primitive times when things were either dangerous and life-threatening or safe. It was far more important to notice the negative things, those things that could potentially harm us, than the positive things because missing the negative things meant we might have missed something that was critical for our survival. By looking for the sabre-toothed tigers in the field rather than the bunny rabbits, we were much more likely to stay alive.

Your brain is still wired in much the same way, so you notice the threatening things, or the 'push away from', a lot more than the 'pull towards'. That's the negativity bias and hypervigilance to threat we discussed in Chapter 5. We just aren't programmed towards positive thinking. In order to rebalance the scales, building awareness of the 'pull towards', or your values and purpose, is a critical step in moving from worry, fear, stress and anxiety into heart-driven, resilient and empowered action.

The values themselves are not a destination. Values are your guiding light – similar to buoy markers on the water – helping to guide you on your life's journey. A good go-to is checking in on what your gut feeling is telling you. It guides you well. Worry tends to be the voice in your head that gets you caught up in self-doubt, second-guessing yourself, checking and rechecking or seeking excessive reassurance. When you check in on what your gut feeling is telling you, it tends to override the critical voice in your head or the voice that says not to do it because something bad might happen.

Your gut feeling is often more in tune with your needs. Fear, on the other hand, takes you on a path away from your values. For example, you might value sharing your knowledge with your friends, but worry then gets in the way and says, 'What if they judge you negatively?' Or you might value giving your best effort and then worry butts in and says, 'Yes, but what if you get it wrong?' Similarly, you might value walks in the fresh air but worry overrides this and says, 'Something bad might happen so don't go.'

Do these kinds of statements sound familiar? Worry is designed to stop all possible bad things from happening, but, in essence, worry stops your fulfilled life from happening. In contrast, your values emanate from your heart. These are the 'pull towards' desired actions and the things in life that give you meaning, purpose, joy and satisfaction. It is these things that you want to build awareness of, and be guided by, in your

actions and interactions in all areas of your life. This is not about throwing caution to the wind – that would more than likely be out of alignment with your values. This is a small pivot that says move out of your head, which is the push away from bad, and move into your heart, which is the pull towards life and fulfilment.

In determining your values, be guided by your gut feeling rather than concern about what you should or shouldn't be – think with your heart.

Gain clarity on your values

Over the years, I have used the following exercise with my clients to help them to build a depth of awareness of and clarity on their personal and professional values. Consider the extent to which each of the values on the following pages are important to you. Place a tick in the box that says whether the value is very important to you, moderately important to you, or not at all important to you.

This is not an exhaustive list. Feel free to add any further values as they come to mind. There is no right or wrong; it's all very personal and everyone is different. Remember that values are not what you are or are not at any one point in time. Rather, values are a guiding direction marking out the way.

To download this values exercise and additional mind strength tools go to drjodie.com.au.

>>

THE ALTERNATIVE TO FEAR-DRIVEN ACTIONS   123

VALUE	Very important	Moderately important	Not at all important
ABUNDANCE – to have a life filled with heart-driven experiences	☐	☐	☐
ACCEPTANCE – to accept the people and experiences around me	☐	☐	☐
ACCOUNTABILITY – to hold true to my commitments	☐	☐	☐
ACCURACY – to be correct or precise	☐	☐	☐
ACHIEVEMENT – to have accomplishments and successes	☐	☐	☐
ADVANCEMENT – to promote a cause or a plan	☐	☐	☐
ADVENTURE – to have daring experiences	☐	☐	☐
ADVOCACY – to demonstrate public support or a cause	☐	☐	☐
AMBITION – to fulfil a strong desire to do or achieve something	☐	☐	☐
APPRECIATION – to recognise and enjoy the good qualities of someone or something	☐	☐	☐
ASSERTIVENESS – to stand up for myself while considering the needs of others	☐	☐	☐
ATTRACTIVENESS – to be appealing to others	☐	☐	☐
AUTHENTICITY – to be honest and real in relationships	☐	☐	☐
AUTHORITY – to have power and control over others	☐	☐	☐
AUTONOMY – to be independent and free from control by others	☐	☐	☐
AWARENESS – to maintain knowledge and perception about myself and others	☐	☐	☐
BALANCE – to create time for the things I have to do and want to do	☐	☐	☐

VALUE	Very important	Moderately important	Not at all important
BEAUTY – to appreciate the qualities around me	☐	☐	☐
BENEVOLENCE – to engage in acts of kindness towards others	☐	☐	☐
BOLDNESS – to take risks and act with confidence or courage	☐	☐	☐
CALMNESS – to be free from agitation or strong emotion	☐	☐	☐
CARING – to display kindness and concern for others	☐	☐	☐
CHALLENGE – to take on situations that stretch my abilities	☐	☐	☐
CHANGE – to enjoy variety in situations and experiences	☐	☐	☐
CHARITY – to give help to those in need	☐	☐	☐
CHEERFULNESS – to embrace life with optimism	☐	☐	☐
CLEVERNESS – to be smart, inventive, wise or witty	☐	☐	☐
COLLABORATION – to work with others to produce something	☐	☐	☐
COMFORT – to have a life with physical and material ease	☐	☐	☐
COMMITMENT – to be dedicated to a cause or activity	☐	☐	☐
COMMUNITY – to engage with other groups with similar attitudes or interests	☐	☐	☐
COMPASSION – to behave with consideration for the wellbeing of myself and others	☐	☐	☐
CONFIDENCE – to have belief in my own abilities	☐	☐	☐
CONSISTENCY – to maintain adherence to the same principles or actions	☐	☐	☐

VALUE	Very important	Moderately important	Not at all important
CONTRIBUTION – to do something for the benefit of others	☐	☐	☐
COOPERATION – to engage with others towards a common goal	☐	☐	☐
COURAGE – to approach things with confidence and bravery	☐	☐	☐
COURTESY – to demonstrate respect for and politeness towards others	☐	☐	☐
CREATIVITY – to express ideas in new ways	☐	☐	☐
CURIOSITY – to have a strong desire to know or learn something	☐	☐	☐
DARING – to be adventurous or bold	☐	☐	☐
DECISIVENESS – to make decisions quickly and effectively	☐	☐	☐
DEDICATION – to be committed to a task or purpose	☐	☐	☐
DEPENDABILITY – to be able to be relied on	☐	☐	☐
DIVERSITY – to have a range of experiences and interests	☐	☐	☐
DUTY – to act in accordance with moral or legal obligations	☐	☐	☐
ECOLOGY – to act with respect for the environment	☐	☐	☐
EMPATHY – to understand and engage with consideration of the feelings of others	☐	☐	☐
ENCOURAGEMENT – to give others support, confidence and hope	☐	☐	☐
ENTHUSIASM – to engage in experiences with enjoyment, interest and approval	☐	☐	☐
ETHICS – to have moral principles governing my behaviour	☐	☐	☐
EXCELLENCE – to have outstanding standards governing my actions	☐	☐	☐

VALUE	Very important	Moderately important	Not at all important
EXCITEMENT – to live life with enthusiasm and thrills	☐	☐	☐
EXPRESSIVENESS – to display meaning and emotion in my actions	☐	☐	☐
FAIRNESS – to provide impartial and just treatment with others	☐	☐	☐
FAITHFULNESS – to have relationships built on loyalty and trust	☐	☐	☐
FAME – to be known by many	☐	☐	☐
FAMILY – to have a cohesive and loving family	☐	☐	☐
FITNESS – to engage in physical activity and be toned or strong	☐	☐	☐
FLEXIBILITY – to be willing to change or compromise when required	☐	☐	☐
FOCUS – to concentrate on a task without distraction	☐	☐	☐
FORGIVENESS – to let go of ill feelings towards others	☐	☐	☐
FREEDOM – to act, speak, or think as I want	☐	☐	☐
FRIENDSHIP – to have amicable, supportive relationships	☐	☐	☐
FUN – to have light-hearted, positive and playful experiences	☐	☐	☐
GENEROSITY – to share in abundance	☐	☐	☐
GENUINENESS – to be authentic and real	☐	☐	☐
GROWTH – to keep developing and evolving	☐	☐	☐
HEALTH – to be free from illness or injury	☐	☐	☐
HELPFULNESS – to be available to support others	☐	☐	☐
HONESTY – to be truthful with myself and others	☐	☐	☐
HOPE – to have positive expectations for the future	☐	☐	☐

>>

VALUE	Very important	Moderately important	Not at all important
HUMILITY – to be humble and modest	☐	☐	☐
HUMOUR – to be amusing or engage in amusing experiences	☐	☐	☐
INCLUSIVENESS – to let people in and make them feel welcome	☐	☐	☐
INDEPENDENCE – to do things for myself	☐	☐	☐
INDIVIDUALITY – to be true to the quality or character that distinguishes me from others	☐	☐	☐
INDUSTRY – to work with diligence and commitment	☐	☐	☐
INNER PEACE – to experience internal tranquillity	☐	☐	☐
INNOVATION – to pursue or create new methods, ideas or products	☐	☐	☐
INSPIRATION – to be stimulated to do something creative	☐	☐	☐
INTEGRITY – to engage ethically and honestly	☐	☐	☐
INTELLIGENCE – to acquire and apply knowledge and skills	☐	☐	☐
INTIMACY – to share intimate connections with others	☐	☐	☐
INTUITION – to understand something instinctively	☐	☐	☐
JOY – to engage in actions that provide feelings of pleasure	☐	☐	☐
JUSTICE – to engage fairly and in line with rules	☐	☐	☐
KINDNESS – to be friendly, generous and considerate	☐	☐	☐
KNOWLEDGE – to have broad awareness of facts and information	☐	☐	☐
LEADERSHIP – to lead a group of people or an organisation	☐	☐	☐

VALUE	Very important	Moderately important	Not at all important
LEARNING – to acquire knowledge or skills through education and experience	☐	☐	☐
LEISURE – to engage in relaxing and rejuvenating activities	☐	☐	☐
LOVE – to share affection with others	☐	☐	☐
LOYALTY – to demonstrate honest allegiance and support to others	☐	☐	☐
MAKING A DIFFERENCE – to have a significant effect on a person, situation or society	☐	☐	☐
MASTERY – to have comprehensive knowledge or skill in a particular area	☐	☐	☐
MINDFULNESS – to embrace the present moment intentionally and without judgement	☐	☐	☐
MODERATION – to avoid extremes in behaviour or opinions and find the middle ground	☐	☐	☐
MONOGAMY – to have only one longstanding intimate partner	☐	☐	☐
MOTIVATION – to pursue activities with enthusiasm	☐	☐	☐
NON-CONFORMITY – to move away from generally accepted ways of engaging or beliefs	☐	☐	☐
NURTURE – to care for and protect others	☐	☐	☐
OPEN-MINDEDNESS – to consider new opinions, ideas or beliefs	☐	☐	☐
ORDER – to be well organised and follow a predetermined routine	☐	☐	☐
PASSION – to have strong feelings or beliefs	☐	☐	☐
PATIENCE – to wait for a desired outcome without becoming agitated	☐	☐	☐

VALUE	Very important	Moderately important	Not at all important
PEACE – to engage in life with tranquility and relaxation	☐	☐	☐
PERSISTENCE – to work with determination towards a goal	☐	☐	☐
PERSONAL DEVELOPMENT – to consciously pursue personal growth	☐	☐	☐
PLAYFULNESS – to be light-hearted or full of fun	☐	☐	☐
PLEASURE – to experience satisfaction and enjoyment	☐	☐	☐
POPULARITY – to be supported and admired by many others	☐	☐	☐
POSITIVITY – to have a positive outlook on experiences and individuals	☐	☐	☐
POWER – to be in a position of influence over others	☐	☐	☐
PREPAREDNESS – to be in a state of readiness	☐	☐	☐
PROACTIVITY – to take control and make things happen	☐	☐	☐
PURPOSE – to have a specific objective that you are working towards	☐	☐	☐
RATIONALITY – to act in accordance with logic	☐	☐	☐
REALISM – to be grounded in practicality and truth	☐	☐	☐
RELATIONSHIPS – to connect with others	☐	☐	☐
RELIABILITY – to be trustworthy or consistent	☐	☐	☐
RELIGION – to act in accordance with my religious beliefs	☐	☐	☐
RESILIENCE – to bounce back from challenges	☐	☐	☐
RESOURCEFULNESS – to find quick and clever ways to resolve situations	☐	☐	☐

VALUE	Very important	Moderately important	Not at all important
RESPONSIBILITY – to be able to be relied upon and accountable for my actions	☐	☐	☐
RESPONSIVENESS – to react easily and readily	☐	☐	☐
RISK – to take chances with the possibility of something bad happening	☐	☐	☐
ROMANCE – to engage in deep and exciting acts of love	☐	☐	☐
SAFETY – to be secure and protected	☐	☐	☐
SELF-ACCEPTANCE – to be kind to and accepting of myself	☐	☐	☐
SELF-CONTROL – to control my own emotions, actions and desires	☐	☐	☐
SELF-ESTEEM – to have self-respect and confidence in my own worth and abilities	☐	☐	☐
SELF-KNOWLEDGE – to know my own values, abilities and emotions	☐	☐	☐
SERVICE – to help or do work for others	☐	☐	☐
SEXUALITY – to have a satisfying sex life	☐	☐	☐
SIMPLICITY – to live life with minimal needs	☐	☐	☐
SOLITUDE – to have my own space away from others	☐	☐	☐
SPIRITUALITY – to be in touch with a deeper sense of meaning or purpose	☐	☐	☐
STABILITY – to have a fairly consistent life	☐	☐	☐
STOICISM – to remain emotionally strong and undisturbed through challenge	☐	☐	☐
SUCCESS – to accomplish an aim or purpose	☐	☐	☐
TEAMWORK – to engage cooperatively with a group	☐	☐	☐
THOUGHTFULNESS – to consider the needs of others	☐	☐	☐

>>

VALUE	Very important	Moderately important	Not at all important
TOLERANCE – to respect differing opinions and behaviours	☐	☐	☐
TRADITION – to follow customs from previous generations	☐	☐	☐
TRANSPARENCY – to be open and honest with nothing to hide	☐	☐	☐
TRUST – to believe in the truth of others	☐	☐	☐
TRUSTWORTHINESS – to be relied on as honest or truthful	☐	☐	☐
UNDERSTANDING – to be sympathetic and tolerant of others	☐	☐	☐
UNIQUENESS – to be one of a kind, special or unusual	☐	☐	☐
VERSATILITY – to adapt to many different functions or activities	☐	☐	☐
VIRTUE – to display high moral standards in my behaviour	☐	☐	☐
VISION – to think or plan for the future	☐	☐	☐
WARMTH – to engage with enthusiasm, affection or kindness	☐	☐	☐
WEALTH – to have an abundance of valuable possessions or money	☐	☐	☐
WELLBEING – to be comfortable, healthy and content	☐	☐	☐
WISDOM – to have experience, knowledge and good judgement	☐	☐	☐
WORLD PEACE – to work towards establishing greater peace and harmony in the world	☐	☐	☐
ZEAL – to have high energy and enthusiasm for a cause	☐	☐	☐
OTHER	☐	☐	☐
OTHER	☐	☐	☐

Of the values you have identified as very important to you, the next step is to write your top 12–15 into the table below. Rate each of these values on relative importance (0 – not at all important; 5 – most important) and alignment. Alignment refers to the extent to which you are living your life aligned with these values (0 – no alignment; 5 – perfect alignment).

VALUE	Importance (0–5)	Alignment (0–5)
1.		
2.		
3.		
4.		
5.		
6.		
7.		
8.		
9.		
10.		
11.		
12.		
13.		
14.		
15.		

>>

>> Gain clarity on your values – continued

Once you have clarity on your values, it is time to move away from fear-driven actions and towards a life of meaning and purpose. In Step 4 of the Mind Strength Method we will turn to building a values-driven action plan involving clarity of purpose, values-driven goals and goal-driven actions so you can move forward aligned with your values with a roadmap for a satisfying life.

Step 2 Summary

Now having finished Step 2 you are able to

1. recognise your worry stories
2. recognise your unhelpful coping strategies
3. recognise that uncertainty and imperfection are normal
4. identify your top core values.

You have tipped the focus from your head and the push away from fear to your heart and your pull towards a life of meaning, purpose and fulfilment.

———

We will now turn to Step 3 of the Mind Strength Method, which will provide you with a Mind Strength Toolkit to make it easier for you to stand up to fear and engage in actions that are aligned with your values. As you know, worry can be very convincing. Worry might say not to do it as something bad will happen, or the critical voice might jump in and say you're not worth it anyway. The Mind Strength Toolkit will make it easier to pivot out of fear and embrace a path of satisfaction, resilience and wellbeing.

STEP

3

The Mind
Strength Toolkit

Chapter 14

A toolkit to build resilience

You are always more powerful than your fear

Congratulations on the work you have done to date to build your mind strength. You now recognise when worry is bossing you around and the negative and catastrophic stories it is trying to tell you. You recognise when the amygdala is trying to assert itself and the physiological sensations of the fight or flight reaction. You know that this is anxiety – helpful in the case of a real threat, but counterproductive in the case of a perceived threat when you are just responding to a worry thought.

You have built awareness of the mental and physical unhelpful coping strategies that can take hold – the 'struggling in quicksand' behaviours you pursue to help yourself but that typically make things worse. You have built awareness of your values. You have tipped the focus from your head to your heart and identified those values that pull you towards a life of meaning, purpose and fulfilment. You are now ready to stand up to fear-driven stories and realign with your values.

The question is how? The amygdala is programmed to hijack our brain and we can lose sight of rational thinking as our prefrontal cortex becomes clouded. Anxiety can also feel awful and scary; we then get anxious about being anxious, tipping anxiety into a panic attack. What hope do we have? The answer is a lot.

I encourage you to feel hopeful and empowered. For a start, you have already built a lot of awareness, which is one of the most powerful tools for finding freedom from anxiety and stress. Anxiety is no longer a mystery. Not only that, you are now aware that anxiety is actually your best friend when you need it – and this is essential because you can now change your relationship with anxiety and loosen its grip a little if you find yourself getting anxious about being anxious.

―――

The chapters ahead are filled with tools built on my years of helping adults, children and adolescents with anxiety. The Mind Strength Toolkit is here to equip you with transformational tools to help you live your life with satisfaction, meaning and success. Together we will progress through the eight tools, practical strategies that will help you to stand up to worry, boss the bully back and move forward aligned with your values. Enjoy.

Chapter 15

TOOL 1

Put the worry story back on the shelf

*Worry is the most predictable fiction
writer of all time: every one of its stories
has an unhappy ending*

One of the most powerful tools in the Mind Strength Toolkit is awareness of your thoughts. So one of the first things you can do is start to get really good at noticing when worry is bossing you around and what it is telling you. As you know, worry plays out like a bully trying to get your attention and trigger an emotional reaction. Reducing the power of worry involves standing up to the bully through building self-awareness as you have already done in Steps 1 and 2. Now, in Step 3, you will use resilience strategies to notice and label that worry story in order to get some distance from it.

Case Study

One of Ella's main worries was the wellbeing of her children. She would get anxious when her 14-year-old daughter, May, was out at a party. Worry started to boss Ella around. Worry is sneaky – it knows how to try to hook you in. Worry played on Ella's vulnerabilities and planted seeds of doubt in her head about the things she held most dear – in this case, her children.

Let's see how this played out for Ella. Her rational mind wanted to argue back. But worry always had a response – it was persistent. Before Ella knew it, her amygdala hijacked her brain and she began freaking out that something terrible had happened to May.
Her internal dialogue went something like this:

Rational mind: I wonder how May is going?
Worry: There are bad people out there. What if something bad has happened to her?

Rational mind: No, of course nothing bad has happened to her, she's just at a party with her friends.
Worry: Yes, but what if she got sidetracked along the way? What if she and her friends are drinking? What if something disastrous has happened?

Rational mind: No, of course nothing disastrous has happened. May is a sensible child; she won't have done anything stupid.
Worry: Yes, but how do you know for sure? Just say something bad has happened ...

Rational mind: Oh, no. Perhaps something bad has happened. I don't know for sure. I know! I can track her phone.

Worry: Yes, but what if something has happened to her and she doesn't have her phone? What if she's drunk and she doesn't know what she's doing?

Rational mind: Goodness, I feel awful. What if something bad has happened? I should have known better. I shouldn't have let her go ...

Amygdala hijack!

● ● ●

At Ella's core are all sorts of powerful, positive personal qualities. Remember, we worry because we care. Years of helping adults, children and adolescents have provided me with more than sufficient evidence to demonstrate this. Anxiety typically brings with it the loveliest of human beings. You are the protector, the leader, the warrior. So, as awful as anxiety can feel at times, you don't want to hate the anxiety. You know where it's coming from – you care because you care.

You now have the self-awareness from Step 1 to recognise that arguing, struggling, trying to push away and challenge the thoughts are mental safety behaviours and make your anxiety feelings worse not better. Instead of getting hooked into worry's tricks of chasing those seeds of doubt with a negative spiral of further worry, one of the most simple, powerful and effective tools in the Mind Strength Toolkit is to start to notice and conceptualise worry thoughts as a boring, predictable story that worry keeps on telling you.

Remember the worry stories from page 95? Your worry stories can typically be grouped into three broad clusters:

1. The 'Something Bad Will Happen' story
2. The 'Outcome Will Be a Catastrophe' story
3. The 'You Won't Be Able to Cope' story.

Case Studies

Luke's worry story was very specific. Worry was telling Luke that a dog was going to attack and hurt him. The story was vivid in his mind: something bad was going to happen, the outcome was going to be a catastrophe and he would not be able to cope. Luke began to notice when this worry story came up in his mind. He was able to practise getting some distance from the story and to boss worry back by noticing and accepting the story as just a story rather than getting hooked in to the content and the details of it. For Luke, the story played out in his mind a little like a scary movie. He was able to start to think of it like a movie that he watched from time to time. Luke and his mum even started to be a bit playful with the concept and, instead of getting hooked in to the content of the story and taking it so seriously, his mum started to respond with humour and spoke about going to make popcorn if he was going to settle in to watching the movie.

Mike had a few stories that were hooking him in to the fight or flight pathway. Specifically, Mike feared that he wouldn't have enough money for the future. Worry tormented him, and the more he got caught up in the content of the story, the worse he felt. On exploring the content of the story a little deeper, we saw that for Mike it was a fear of not being able to provide for his family that resonated more strongly – a fear of failure. In essence, his struggle was clearly a battle with uncertainty and his deep desire to have certainty and control. Noticing it as the 'Financial Failure' story was a helpful strategy for Mike. It enabled him to get some distance from the worry thoughts as they came up. He understood that every chapter in that story was simply his attempt to gain certainty when there was no certainty – so the story served no useful purpose.

The second story that played out in Mike's life was the 'Health Problem' story. Again, it was Mike's persistent worry bossing him around, telling him that he had to know for sure. It tipped him into hypervigilance to threat, the negativity bias and a whole realm of checking and reassurance-seeking safety behaviours. By noticing the story when it came up and putting the book back on the shelf, Mike was able to not get hijacked by his amygdala. By doing things such as having regular meetings with his accountant and ensuring financial management of the things that were in his control, he was able to return to values-aligned vigilance, not fear-driven hypervigilance (see page 37) and get on with enjoying his life.

Ella's story was one of perfectionism. Although worry told Ella that she was not a good mum and not a good leader at work, in essence the underlying belief that worry told Ella was that she had to be perfect in order to be okay: the 'Perfection' story. Ella found it incredibly helpful to notice when this story book came off the shelf. She was able to start to identify it, accept it as a story then put it gently and compassionately back on the shelf.

Allie's story was similar to Ella's in that she also felt that she needed to be perfect in order to be okay. However, for Allie, her worry story was specifically around the fear of being judged negatively. On the back of childhood bullying, Allie was terrified of doing the wrong thing by others, not being accepted or not being seen to be good enough in some way. Allie decided that her worry story was the 'Negative Judgement' story. On getting some distance from the story, Allie recognised that the one who was the most brutal bully in negative judgement was indeed herself or the critical voice inside her mind. By noticing when the 'Negative Judgement' story book had come off the shelf, she was able to gently and compassionately close the book and put it back on the shelf. She recognised that the content of the story was taking her right away from a values-driven path and served no effective purpose for where she wanted to go in life.

Adam's story was clear. He feared that he would not be good enough at his schoolwork and, ultimately, he feared failure. Worry and the resulting anxiety had tipped him into all sorts of flight and fight behaviours. The 'I Will Fail' story had taken hold. The challenge for Adam was that gaming addiction and digital distraction had kicked in as strong and stubborn flight behaviours, which then reinforced the story. However, once Adam was able to notice the worry story and bring the focus away from outcome and back to effort, he felt more empowered to approach his studies and let go of his safety behaviours. The 'I Will Fail' story' had kept Adam trapped in procrastination, but now it was time for him to reclaim his power.

Name your worry story

Have a think about the last time worry was bossing you around. What story was worry telling you? If that story was a book, what title would you give it? Think about that title right now. For example:

- The 'I'm Not Good Enough' story
- The 'Negative Judgement' story
- The 'I Will Fail' story
- The 'Spider Will Kill Me' story
- The 'I'm an Imposter' story
- The 'I Can't Trust Them' story

Whatever the book is, I'd imagine you've read it many, many times, right? And guess who the author is? That's right – worry! Sometimes worry will read you Chapter 1, other times it will be Chapter 2, or Chapter 3 and then it might be Chapter 1 again. You've read the book so many times that it's actually boring! Sometimes the worry story keeps the same theme, just the characters or location or content change a little.

>>

When you open the book and start reading the pages, how does it make you feel? Does reading the book help in any way at all? No. It's a totally unhelpful story that only makes you feel stressed out, upset and anxious.

It is not about challenging the story or arguing with the content. Remember that if you try to do that, you'll typically find any attempts to hook in to the content of the worry thoughts just dig you deeper into your worries – often at 2 am when all you want to do is sleep. As you know, arguing with the content of the worry thoughts is one of the tricks that worry uses to draw you in and make worry even more powerful.

Do you want to hate worry? Definitely no – worry isn't to be hated; after all, it's just thoughts in your mind. You don't want to get angry when worry has taken the book off the bookshelf. When you hate worry or get angry with it, it takes you on the anger and aggression pathway that also keeps the amygdala firing, that part of your brain that's revving you up in fight or flight. This, in turn will activate hypervigilance to threat and will keep you focused on your worries. All you want to do is notice worry as the bully it is and not give it the attention it's demanding from you. You turn your attention back towards the things that you want to do and not the things worry is telling you to do. Instead, employ the following steps.

1. Notice when the book has come off the bookshelf.
2. Label it as the worry story – 'I know you, you're the "I'm Not Good Enough" story' (or any other worry story that's relevant).

>>

3. Gently and compassionately imagine closing the book and putting it back on the shelf.
4. Take a long, slow breath out to create the space to choose a values-driven action as an alternative.
5. Continue on with your day (or night!), doing something that is values-driven, not fear-driven.

It is just about noticing, observing, allowing. Then realigning with your values, your purpose, your strategy, your values-driven goals and actions. (More about this coming up.)

Turn the attention back to what you want to do, not what worry is telling you to do. Sure, worry might try to get you to read the story again. But you now know exactly what to do – you just need to follow the steps above.

Thoughts are just thoughts

So what then does worry become if not this all-important, all-knowing voice in our head? Basically, worry just becomes thoughts. One of your superpowers in standing up to worry is to recognise that worry in fact has no power at all because worry is, well, nothing more than just thoughts. Let's have a think about this for a second.

How many thoughts do you have in any one day? What do you think – 600? 6000? Although estimates vary, some research has found that the human mind can experience approximately 60,000 thoughts in a day. SIXTY THOUSAND! Hard to believe, huh?

Whether it's 6,000 or 60,000 thoughts, which ones do we tend to remember? That's right, we remember the worry ones: the ones that say you're going to mess up that presentation, or you will say something stupid, or they won't like you at the event so don't go, or some other bad, dangerous thing will happen. Due to our inherent negativity bias and hypervigilance to threat, we let ourselves get bossed around by a mere portion of these 60,000 thoughts. Yet they are all the same. They are all. Just. Thoughts.

Let's take a moment to think about what thoughts are.

- Thoughts are just sentences.
- Sentences are just words.
- Words are just letters.
- Letters are just shapes.
- Shapes are just neural impulses in our brain!

That's right – we let ourselves be bossed around by random neural impulses creating shapes in our mind. We let these shapes in our mind determine whether we feel happy or sad, powerful or weak, scared, angry or calm.

Often, we get hooked in to the content of these negative thoughts without much concrete evidence to support them. We follow negative thoughts with more negative thoughts and this triggers the fight or flight reaction. Once fight or flight is activated, our rational mind then becomes less accessible, we become hijacked by our amygdala and it becomes even more difficult to get out of this negative spiral. The snowball builds up and before we know it, we're a stressed-out mess!

The good news is that you can always feel empowered. You can choose whether to listen to the worry thoughts or not. Worry actually has no power unless you let it have power. You can always create the space to choose whether to get sucked into the vortex of the worry thoughts, self-doubt thoughts, critical thoughts or negative thoughts – or whether you take a different path instead. You always have a choice.

Keep in mind that to some degree you are changing a mental habit here, and that habit is worry. As you know, habits are challenging to break; however, with motivation, determination, consistency and persistence, habits are well and truly breakable. Remember, worry will try to trick you into thinking that the outcome will be a disaster. Accept this as another one of worry's tricks and practise putting that old, familiar storybook back on the shelf.

Of the worry thoughts that are in your control, you want to tip your mind from focusing on the problem to focusing on the solution. A solution focus means that you engage in problem-solving and action-planning around the things that *are* within your control. That's vastly different from just dwelling on your worries. We'll look into this more in Chapter 18.

Chapter 16

TOOL 2

Dissolve the amygdala hijack through mindfulness

Create the space to choose values over fear

In order to have the clarity to choose values over fear, you need to first learn ways to quieten your amygdala and take yourself out of fight or flight. This typically is not easy, as in essence you are overriding your primitive biological instincts. As we know, the amygdala is pre-programmed to hijack your brain. If you are in a real life or death situation, you want to be able to access your survival instinct and run away or fight to keep yourself alive. However, in the case of a perceived threat, or worry thought, the alarm bell doesn't need to fire – it's basically a false alarm, responding only because worry is telling it to. So we need to learn ways to quieten it.

Stop

Take long slow out-breaths

Observe your surroundings

Proceed

A powerful tool in the Mind Strength Toolkit to quieten the hijacking amygdala is a four-step process called the STOP Strategy.

Step 1: Stop and stand up to the hijacking amygdala

The amygdala is designed to take over with sudden and immediate urgency, so you need to first halt it in its tracks. This is not an easy task. As your brain is pre-programmed to be hijacked by the amygdala in order to keep you alert and alive in situations of real threat, you need to be quite purposeful in standing up to it. You now know that you can only change what you are aware of in the first place. So awareness of when the amygdala starts to fire – and what that feels like specifically for you – will allow you to take effective action.

When the amygdala starts to fire, your sympathetic nervous system and the fight or flight reaction are activated. This brings with it a whole cluster of physiological sensations, all of which make sense in the context of your body helping you to fight or to run in dangerous situations, but unhelpful in response to a perceived threat. Have a think about what physiological sensations show up for you.

- Does your heart rate start to increase?
- Does your breath start to become rapid and shallow?
- Do your muscles start to clench up?
- Do you feel light-headed?
- Do you feel tingly or electric feelings in your arms or legs?
- Do you go into fight mode with its physiological sensations and get angry for having them?
- Do you start to get stressed about feeling stressed?
- Does the worry story start to hijack your brain and get you to focus in on it and then start to chase it with more worry and fear?

Notice when worry is starting to boss you around and take immediate action by saying STOP. As worry will try to be very convincing in bossing you around, it is good for you to be quite strong in standing up to it. Lean into awareness of those bodily sensations – notice them and recognise them as the hijacking amygdala. Then move to Step 2.

Step 2: Take a few long, slow out-breaths

Let's focus in on what typically happens with your breath when the sympathetic nervous system is activated. Adrenaline makes your heart rate increase and your breathing become rapid and shallow. This serves to oxygenate your muscles as your body primes itself to defend itself and stay alive. How do you breathe in order to stand up to the hijacking amygdala?

Traditionally, calm-down breathing is all about breathing deeply. 'Just breathe deeply and you'll be okay', right? The challenge, however, is that when the amygdala is firing and the sympathetic nervous system is activated, the muscles in your body, chest and abdomen become tense. Breathing deeply when muscle tension is taking hold typically results in a feeling that you can't get the air in – that you can't breathe. In this context, deep breathing can actually exacerbate the anxiety. You might be inclined to interpret these physiological experiences in a catastrophic way and get anxious about the feeling of not being able to breathe, which triggers more fight or flight, and this can end up spiralling into a panic attack.

So, instead of trying to breathe in and struggling, you want to do the opposite – you want to take a long, slow out-breath. The best way to do this is through pursed lips.

MIND STRENGTH ACTION

Practise a long, slow out-breath

Think about something hot that you enjoy either eating or drinking. Perhaps it's pumpkin soup or a cup of tea. Imagine it is just a little too hot to eat or drink and you need to cool it down. That's the kind of long, slow out-breath that you want to be doing. See how you go in practising it now. Visualise cooling down the cup of tea. Or perhaps you can visualise blowing out some birthday candles or blowing some bubbles – a long, slow out-breath will help you to bring yourself back to the present moment and take you out of the fight or flight reaction.

As you breathe out, see if you can notice where in your body the muscle tension or physiological experiences of anxiety are and breathe through them, observe them and allow them to just be. You don't want to fight them, hate them or try to get rid of them. You just want to notice them and create space, kindness and love around them. Once you have completed your long, slow out-breath, just let your lungs fill up naturally without doing anything purposeful with the in-breath – just let the lungs do what they want to do.

If you enjoy visualisation, you can add to this breathing exercise the following visualisation:

- With every out-breath you are blowing the worry, stress, agitation, low mood or distress away. You can observe and notice the letters of the word 'worry' or 'fear' or 'anxiety' (or whatever word is relevant to you) being blown away with every out-breath.
- Build in a pause between the out-breath and the in-breath.
- With every in-breath you can visualise scooping up the muscle tension wherever it sits in your body and letting it go and dissolve with every out-breath.

Remember, start with the out-breath – blow the stress away. Build in a pause between the out-breath and the in-breath. With your in-breath, just let your lungs fill up naturally.

Your body can trick your brain

The STOP strategy is all about biofeedback to your brain. Your brain is very used to certain things happening in association with one another. For example, the neurochemicals in your brain send messages to your body to have tight muscles and rapid, shallow breathing, which then become associated with feeling anxious. With biofeedback, instead of your brain giving your body instructions to engage in a particular way, you can use your body to influence your brain. Biofeedback to the brain says that the best way to tell the brain that anxiety is not needed right now is to slow your breathing down. By doing this you are overriding the hijacking amygdala. You are tricking your brain into taking you out of the fight or flight response, and this turns off the alarm and calms down your reaction.

Step 3: Observe what's going on around you

As you know, typically, when you're in fight or flight mode your brain is focused in on what you feel threatened by – creating hypervigilance to threat. This might be a strong internal focus, either on the anxiety feelings or on the worry thoughts. Worry takes you into all sorts of negative possibilities about the future – often this is catastrophising, or focusing on the worst-case scenario. For example, you might be worrying about how you're coming across, about whether you'll make a fool of yourself, whether your words will come out correctly, whether you'll look strange or embarrassing or whether something dangerous will happen in a particular situation. Alternatively, your mind might be focused in on fear-driven behaviours. For example, you might be working out an escape plan for how you might exit the restaurant if you start feeling sick.

This internal fear-driven focus keeps the anxiety alive. All of the great work that's being undertaken in long, slow out-breaths will be undermined if your prefrontal cortex is still focusing in on your source of perceived threats and retriggering the hijacking amygdala.

The key to success, therefore, is turning the attention outwards and observing what's going on around you. This is powerful, mindful engagement. By purposefully focusing on the present moment, you are, by default, taking your attention away from the worry thoughts and concerns about the future. Action actually involves the opposite of what you might think. It's not struggling with the worry thoughts or trying to block the worry thoughts as in the pink elephant experiment on page 104; it's simply noticing the worry thoughts, labelling them as worry and bringing your thoughts back to the present moment through purposeful observation.

Similarly, you might think that if your amygdala is trying to hijack your brain, you should fight it and struggle with it. The byproduct of this is getting angry, frustrated or disappointed with yourself for feeling anxious. You might tell yourself that you're useless, too sensitive or no good. This form of 'invalidating' your own emotions only serves to ignite the amygdala further. So how do you let the amygdala feel heard while not buying in to it? You actually want to accept it. That's right: the best way to quieten the hijacking amygdala is, in fact, to accept it, to observe it, to allow it, with non-judgemental curiosity.

This is mindfulness. The essence of mindfulness is intentionally observing and allowing both your internal and your external experiences to just be, with non-judgemental curiosity. It is

- present moment awareness
- observing
- allowing
- intentional
- non-judgemental.

You observe the physical sensations of the amygdala with no objective or goal – simply to observe, to be, and to allow. While accepting the amygdala and the sensations of anxiety, you breathe 'alongside' the fight or flight reaction, rather than breathing to 'get rid of' the fight or flight reaction – you observe and allow as you engage in this breathing.

Acceptance is the opposite of struggle – and it's the struggle that keeps you in fight or flight. So experiment with sitting with the discomfort of uncertainty. Maybe the feelings will stop and maybe they won't. When you sit with the uncertainty, observe and allow rather than struggle and fight, you encounter the paradoxical effect of the emotions decreasing rather than increasing their power. It's when you take yourself out of the boxing ring with the feelings that the feelings actually dissolve. The amygdala feels heard and the alarm is turned off.

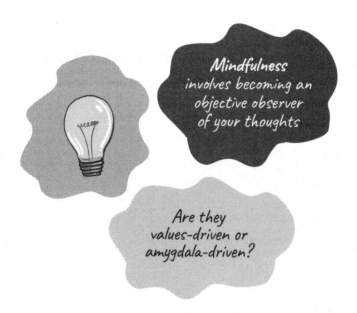

Mindfulness involves becoming an objective observer of your thoughts

Are they values-driven or amygdala-driven?

Alongside observing and allowing the sensations of the fight or flight reaction and breathing through them without struggle, you want to adopt a similar strategy with your thoughts. This involves being the objective observer of your thoughts. Can you experiment with keeping a bit of distance from your thoughts, viewing them as if they are separate from you?

Can you imagine that your thoughts are like subtitles on a movie screen? Just like watching a movie or reading a book, the subtitles might trigger an emotional reaction, but ultimately you know that they are not you – they are just a script that is playing out in your mind.

In getting distance from your thoughts, you are allowing yourself to be a more objective observer. You can then apply the Mind Strength Method and ask yourself whether the thoughts are fear-driven or values-driven.

Focus on the five senses

An easy go-to for purposeful observation in the present moment is to turn the spotlight outwards, away from the worry thoughts, and actively focus on each of the five senses.

• What can you see around you?
• What can you hear around you?
• What can you touch around you?
• What can you taste?
• What can you smell?

This is the essence of mindfulness. It is a powerful tool to stand up to the hijacking amygdala and re-engage the parasympathetic nervous system. A good way to practise mindful engagement of the five senses is through daily mindful walking. See if you can walk around the block with the intention of checking in on whatever senses are relevant to you in the present moment. Slow your breathing down through purposeful action, notice when the thoughts come up, let them float on by, and re-engage in your surroundings. See page 165 for more on attention training.

STEP 4: Proceed, ensuring values-driven action

Once you have stopped, taken a few long, slow out-breaths and observed the five senses around you, you have rescued your hijacked brain and are in a calmer state. You are then ready to go to 'P'. This, quite simply, refers to proceed with what you were doing before the anxiety took hold. See if you can take purposeful action in a values-driven direction.

Extra layering of emotions

Remember, the key to the Mind Strength Method is recognising that the situation is not always in your control; however, you can choose how you respond to that situation. This applies to your thoughts, feelings and actions. For example, imagine that you tripped over and broke your arm. Now it's sore and in a cast. How might you respond to that painful, broken arm?

You might choose to get angry at the fact that it's broken. Things have been going well, you have some projects on at work, at university or school, life is taking hold, you have lots to do, and now you've gone and broken your arm. So, alongside the anger, you experience frustration at your broken arm. Your frustration and anger result in hypervigilance to the broken arm – you focus in on your arm, which exacerbates your perception of the pain. The negativity bias now kicks in. You start to feel worried and begin to think about all of the possible things that might go wrong. Worry starts telling you the 'It's Going to be a Catastrophe' story, 'it will never mend', 'you will lose your job', 'you won't get the things done that you need to get done'. Anxiety starts to take hold. The hijacking amygdala triggers increased muscle tension around the broken arm, which in turn increases your pain. As the pain intensifies, your mood declines. Sadness starts to intensify into depression. Depression results in you withdrawing from activities and shutting down from getting out into nature, catching up with your friends and doing valued activities. And so it goes ...

Retrain your brain

The wonderful thing about the brain is that it is constantly changing and adapting in response to your environmental experiences. This is called neuroplasticity. Your brain is continually establishing new neural networks that are adapting and evolving based on new learning. As a result, it's entirely possible to rewire your brain to spend more time observing and allowing your experiences in the present moment. A Mind Strength Action for facilitating this process is called attention training.

Train your attention

Attention training involves finding a neutral activity two or more times a day and observing the five senses as you engage in that activity. Remember the Mind Strength Action on page 162? For example, the activity might be drinking a cup of tea. Engaging the senses in the present moment would involve drinking that cup of tea and with each sip running through what you can see, hear, touch, taste and smell. As you go through each of those senses, practise simply observing and allowing the experiences of those senses in the present moment. It is not about judging those senses, such as 'this tea tastes nice'; it is simply being in the moment with those senses. If you notice a judgement thought come into your mind, simply notice the thought, observe it and allow it to just float on by like clouds in the sky.

As you know, every time you try to control your thoughts, or push them out of your mind or struggle with them, the thoughts will dig in more strongly. The struggle, blocking or attempting to get rid of the thoughts, is what keeps you trapped in them. The noticing, observing, allowing and just letting them be is what helps the thoughts to float on by.

When you practise this, you can start to apply the same exercise to noticing, observing and allowing the worry thoughts, and worry story, to float on by when they come up rather than getting hooked in to the content of the thoughts, resulting in the worry snowball taking hold.

>>

What neutral activities can you use to practise attention training? Examples include focusing on the five senses while you are

- having breakfast, lunch or dinner
- in the shower
- brushing your teeth
- brushing your hair
- sitting on the bus or train
- walking in the park or to work or school
- sipping a glass of water.

There are so many actions you can do on a daily basis that would be great to experiment with as attention training exercises. See if you can build them into your day, and enjoy moving from anxiety and stress into practical and resilient action.

Chapter 17

TOOL 3

Get out of the boxing ring with uncertainty

Sitting with uncertainty rather than fighting it
is your greatest chance of success

As you know from Step 1 of the Mind Strength Method, humans don't like uncertainty. This goes back to our cave-dwelling days, when a sabre-toothed tiger might be lurking around the corner, ready to gobble us up. Predictability equals safety – if you have predictability you can remain in control and, in doing so, ensure that nothing bad is going to happen.

This is where worry comes in like a wolf in sheep's clothing, telling you that it is going to sort it all out for you. Worry says that the more you struggle with the fear, the closer you'll come to certainty. And worry is very convincing. So you listen. You get hooked in to the worry spiral and grapple with uncertainty, trying to make sure that nothing bad happens – trying to get certainty. It's as if you're in a heavyweight boxing championship. You're in the boxing ring and your opponent is uncertainty. You fight, and fight, and fight. But your opponent is a force that you can't compete with – your opponent always wins. And why? There is no certainty. There will never be certainty.

The problem with being in the boxing ring with uncertainty is that not only are you fighting a battle that you will never win, but the very nature of being in the boxing ring is keeping your amygdala activated – you are caught in the sympathetic nervous system, and adrenaline and cortisol are surging through your bloodstream. This gets to the heart of anxiety. Your struggle with uncertainty is one of the strongest triggers of your survival instinct, and while you remain in that boxing ring you will keep that brain alarm on.

Sitting with uncertainty

The key to success starts with the letter A, and the word is acceptance. You accept the inevitability of uncertainty. It allows you to pivot and realign with a values-driven path. You recognise that it is a boxing match you will never win because you can never entirely predict the future. There will always be some element of uncertainty, and while you are struggling to eliminate uncertainty you keep the anxiety alive. So you step out of the boxing ring and, instead, allow yourself to sit with the discomfort of uncertainty. This builds up your resilience and reduces your fight or flight reaction.

Now, don't get me wrong, this is not about giving up hope about your power to make a difference. This is just about refocusing your energy to areas where you have control.

So, next time worry suggests you get into the boxing ring with uncertainty, stand up to worry and purposefully lean into uncertainty instead. Purposefully allow exposure to the concept of uncertainty, and sit with the discomfort of uncertainty rather than getting rid of it or trying to reassure your way around it. Say things like

Maybe it will and maybe it won't.
Maybe it is and maybe it isn't.
Maybe they do and maybe they don't.

Focus on problem-solving in the present moment. When you purposefully allow yourself to sit with the discomfort of uncertainty rather than get rid of it, over time you will watch your anxiety dissolve.

Chapter 18

TOOL 4

Move from worry to problem-solving

Tipping the focus from outcome to effort

Fundamental to the Mind Strength Method is moving from the fight or flight pathway towards a values-driven pathway. This is the difference between hypervigilance, which is typically fear-driven, and vigilance, which is typically values-driven. When you are vigilant, you are pulled towards values such as safety, love, protection, health and wellbeing. Instead of the worry and catastrophising that can occur with hypervigilance, when your thoughts, feelings and actions are aligned with values-driven vigilance, you engage in problem-solving and action-planning.

Let's take a closer look. You value the wellbeing of your family so you maintain vigilance and engage in practical actions to ensure the security, health and happiness of your loved ones.

Associated actions might include eating balanced, healthy meals, taking your children to the doctor if they are sick, wearing sunscreen at the beach and teaching your children to look both ways before they cross the road. For example, if your 13-year-old son is going out on the weekend, you would engage in prudent practical action to manage his wellbeing. You might stay abreast of what the experts are suggesting regarding cyber safety and teen mental health, you might seek clarity regarding your son's plans and who he is going to be with, you might equip him with a phone so that he is contactable, and you might text the parent of the friend he is going to be with.

In contrast, when you are fear-driven an instinctive hyper-vigilance kicks in. You worry about all the things that might go wrong. You are more inclined to start to engage in fear-driven actions. For example, you might try to get certainty through over-checking, avoiding, overprotecting and worrying.

Hypervigilance is intolerance of uncertainty, resulting in an abundance of safety behaviours to rule out any chance that something bad will happen. The challenge and where you become trapped is searching for certainty where there is none – so you are setting yourself up for failure right from the start. You become caught in a whirlwind of anxiety through your own hypervigilance.

This is not about throwing caution to the wind. Of course, you want to keep yourself, your family and your friends safe, flourishing and satisfied. It is not a perfect world, and, in this imperfect world where negative things do still happen, the important consideration is whether you can respond to a situation with values-driven vigilance rather than fear-driven hypervigilance.

So, short of keeping your children at home or checking and rechecking where they are, struggling to get certainty keeps us trapped in the fight or flight. We are now no longer engaging in values-driven actions to keep our family happy and well, we are engaging in fear-driven actions to avoid uncertainty. What we need to do is shift the focus from hypervigilance, worry and needing certainty, to vigilance, problem-solving and sitting with the discomfort of uncertainty.

From outcome to effort

Part of the discomfort with uncertainty and worry is focusing on outcome – you must know what the outcome will be, and it must be perfect. This is giving away your power to worry and keeping you trapped in anxiety. You strive for a certain outcome, which is striving to achieve the unachievable.

A helpful alternative is to build self-awareness, notice when your mind has jumped to outcome, and bring it back to a focus on effort. Outcome is out of your control, whereas effort is in your control. Critical to your resilience and your sense of well-being is a three-step process:

1. Notice when your mind is focusing on outcome.
2. Bring the focus back to effort.
3. Be proud of yourself for that effort.

Postpone your worry and focus on solutions

There is a powerful, practical strategy that you can engage in to help you to overcome hypervigilance and fear-driven action. As you know, the first step is to become proficient at recognising what worry looks and sounds like. You can even consider giving worry a name.

STEP 1: Note down the worry thoughts as they arise

What is worry telling you? Note it down in a journal or the Notes app on your phone. As you know, worry is like a snowball rolling down a mountain – the more attention you give it the larger it gets! By noting down the worry thoughts as they arise you can get a bit of distance from the content of the thoughts and stop them from spiralling out of control.

STEP 2: At a specific time each day, spend 15–20 minutes attending to your list

Attend to your worry list at a certain time each day, ideally in the late afternoon. If worry is proving to be very stubborn and problematic, particularly at night, you can do this step twice a day. This might be once in the morning and once in the afternoon. There is no right or wrong, so think about what works best for you and factor it into every day. When you attend to your list you want to differentiate between:

a. **Items that are no longer relevant**

   What do you do with the items that are no longer relevant? That's right, just delete them or cross them out.

For example, you might have been worrying about a disagreement you had with a work colleague and later that day the two of you ended up going out for lunch together and made up. No need to dwell on something that's resolved – delete!

b. **Items that are out of your control**

For example, you might be worrying about whether you've done well enough on an assignment or work submission. Worrying about things that are out of your control is a futile effort, serving no purpose other than using up your mental energy and making you feel terrible. Yet, when we struggle with uncertainty, we spend so much of our day dwelling on things that we are simply unable to do anything about.

c. **Items that are in your control**

These are the kinds of thoughts that you can do something about. For example, you might be worrying about asking your boss for a pay increase or concerned about a fight you had with your partner or friend.

d. **Items where you are focusing on outcome**

Focusing on outcomes can be a trigger for stress and anxiety due to discomfort with uncertainty, so it's helpful to identify thoughts where you are focusing on the outcome and practise bringing the focus back to effort. When outcomes are out of your control, focusing on effort brings you one step closer to engaging in problem-solving and action-planning around the elements that are in your control.

>>

STEP 3: Practise mindfulness strategies to let go of the items that are out of your control

For these thoughts, it is helpful to engage in strategies that assist in letting go of the worry. This one works well: visualise a leaf floating down a beautiful stream. Wrap up that worry thought in a bundle, place it on the leaf and let it float away – it can even go all the way down a waterfall if you choose.

STEP 4: Convert worry into problem-solving

Of the worry thoughts that are in your control, you want to tip your mind away from focusing on the problem to focusing on the solution. A solution focus means that you engage in problem-solving and action-planning. That is vastly different from just dwelling on your worries. Where worry leads to more worry, problem-solving leads to solutions!

The problem-solving process is very straightforward and involves the following steps:

1. Specify the problem in concrete, solution-focused terms.
2. Brainstorm solutions.
3. Develop an action plan.
4. Implement the plan.
5. Review and revise the plan as required.

In one of our sessions, Ella reported that her husband had been going through a significantly stressful period at work. There were substantial cost-cutting measures, which had resulted in his job being made redundant. This was causing Ella a lot of stress. She worried that he wouldn't find a new job in a tough market for his profession. It was causing her sleepless nights as her fear of uncertainty started to take hold. She wore the weight of her husband's stress on her shoulders and she wanted to alleviate his pain.

This experience, among others, proved an excellent opportunity for Ella to practise the postponing worry, problem-solving and action-planning strategies. Each day, Ella noticed the worry thoughts as they came to mind. Instead of chasing them with more worries, she wrote down the thoughts in the Notes app on her phone. This stopped the snowballing of worry in its tracks.

Ella found that the same, or similar, worry thoughts often came up – thoughts about not being good enough at home and work, about being judged negatively, about not doing enough, about the wellbeing of her children and husband. She found it particularly helpful to note down the worry thoughts that came up at night because she felt that they were now captured and that she would be able to attend to them in her own time. She was reclaiming her power over worry, rather than giving in to the power that worry previously had over her.

Each day at around 4 pm, and sometimes also at around 10 am if she'd had a particularly challenging night, Ella attended to her worry list by sorting the items into four different categories:

1. Items that were no longer relevant.
2. Items that were in her control.
3. Items that were out of her control.
4. Items that were outcome based.

Some things on her list were partially in her control and partially out of her control.

Converting worry into problem-solving allowed Ella to gain some objectivity on her thoughts and to recognise that there was no point dwelling on the things that were out of her control – worry served no purpose.

With practice, Ella became better and better at letting go of the worries relating to things that were out of her control. She allowed herself to sit with the discomfort of uncertainty. She was also able to recognise the particular worry stories that tended to come up on repeat. She wrapped those worries into a book that she titled the 'Not Good Enough' story and put that book back on the bookshelf. She became good at recognising that the specific worries on her worry list were commonly just different chapters of the one overarching boring, unhelpful story – a story that served no purpose other than making her feel anxious, stressed and exhausted.

There were, however, thoughts that came up that were certainly in her control. For these thoughts, Ella applied the problem-solving strategy. For example, Ella worried about her husband's redundancy. The stream of worry thoughts that came up sounded a little like this:

- What will that mean about our livelihood?
- Will we be able to keep the kids in the schools they are in?

- What if it takes him ages to find a new job?
- What if he never finds a new job?
- How will others perceive him?
- Will they think that he is stupid?
- Will our friends reject us?
- What will the stress do for our marriage?
- What if he can't cope with it all?
- What if he gets depressed?
- How will I then cope?
- I need him to be my rock – what if he gets super stressed and is no longer able to manage?

Ella recognised that a lot of her worry thoughts around this issue were out of her control. There were, however, areas where she could apply substantial problem-solving and action-planning. Specifically, her problem-solving looked a little like this:

1. Specify the problem in solution-oriented terms
- Help my husband to find a job and map out a financial plan to maximise financial stability.

2. Brainstorm solutions and develop action plan
- Review the financials and our monthly budget.
- Identify and reduce non-essential spends in the short term.
- Meet with our accountant.
- Follow up leads in my social media network.
- Contact my friend to help my husband with his job search.
- Practise self-kindness and recognise that this is my husband's task, not mine. I will help wherever I can.

3. Review and revise as necessary

By focusing on problem-solving, not worry, Ella had more energy and resilience to be the supportive, loving partner she enjoyed being. Support and love were values-driven and not driven by fear of not being good enough. She had turned anxiety into empowerment through engaging with this helpful, practical strategy. She and her husband were able to work as a team to help him to find a new job as soon as possible.

Chapter 19

TOOL 5

Approach avoided situations

Moving from anticipation into action

When people go down the fear-driven pathway, one of the most common safety behaviours, or unhelpful coping strategies, they engage in is avoidance. This is the essence of the 'flight' in the fight or flight reaction. It makes sense that if your brain is interpreting a perceived threat as if it were a real threat, your survival instinct kicks in to tell you to avoid it. However, when you allow worry to boss you around, you will be more inclined to stay in your cosy little comfort zone and miss out on living the fulfilled life that you deserve. Being bossed around by fear and avoidance leads to dissatisfaction, where you watch life slip by and wish that you could do all sorts of values-driven things that worry is telling you not to do.

Although anxiety affects all of us as a normal part of being human, sometimes the thought of approaching certain avoided situations can be terrifying. This is the Anticipation Zone. This is one of worry's tricks that keeps you trapped.

The Anticipation Zone is often the worst bit. Worry says avoid, avoid, avoid. Worry says don't even think of approaching because something disastrous will happen. Worry builds up this big avoidance hump – so big that it can feel like you're about to climb Mount Everest if you even dare to leave the Anticipation Zone. The problem is when you stay trapped in anticipation, you never allow yourself to get to the Actual Zone. You never allow yourself to learn that worry was wrong, that it wasn't bad at all, or even if something doesn't go completely according to plan it wasn't a catastrophe, and you built up the resilience strategies to cope. So you stay trapped in the Anticipation Zone, fearful of the possibility of something terrible happening if you enter the Actual Zone.

However, the Actual Zone is where the fun lies – it's where you live a life aligned with your values, a life of meaning, purpose and fulfilment. The only way of learning that the Anticipation Zone is worse than the Actual Zone is to approach rather than avoid it. It is to climb what might, at first, feel like Mount Everest and learn through experience that worry was wrong.

The good news is that Mount Everest is not a mountain at all. This is one of worry's tricks. Mount Everest is actually just like a mound of dirt – and every time you approach rather than avoid, that mound gets flatter and flatter, easier and easier. Before you know it, the path is a well-worn track and you are moving from Anticipation into Actual with greater familiarity and ease.

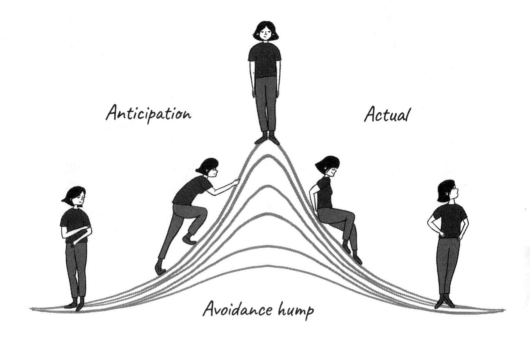

Anticipation

Actual

Avoidance hump

A pivotal tool in the Mind Strength Toolkit is to ever so gradually approach avoided situations. The beauty of this is that when you approach feared situations gradually and take tiny steps out of your comfort zone, you allow yourself to learn that

1. the bad thing didn't happen
2. even if things didn't go perfectly to plan, the outcome wasn't a catastrophe
3. you coped better than you thought you would – worry was tricking you.

The other powerful thing that happens when you face your fears rather than avoid them is that you are not just taking steps out of your comfort zone but, rather, creating a new, larger comfort zone. You get used to the situation and it no longer seems as scary.

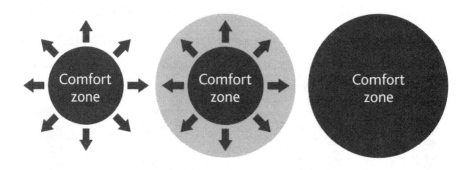

Getting used to the water at the beach

A good analogy is thinking of this process like getting used to the water at the beach. When you first put your toe in the water, it can feel freezing and unpleasant, but then what happens? You get used to it and are ready to take another small step in, and another, and another, every time getting used to the experience that only a short time earlier was unpleasant. Finally, you are ready to plunge right in and experience swimming in the water to its full extent.

As with moving out of the Anticipation Zone and into the Actual Zone, you get used to the previously avoided situation. Taking steps to gradually approach these situations allows you to lay down new learning. What you previously had assumed was terrifying becomes okay – you build up mind strength through approaching instead of avoiding.

Stepping out of your comfort zone

When you've been giving worry attention for a long time, like any bully it has gained a lot of power. So at first the bully is large, and its voice is menacing. The concept of taking big leaps to stand up to worry and fear can be terrifying. This is not what you want. It's really about going at whatever pace works for you that only causes some mild to moderate discomfort or distress. Let's say a 30/100 in discomfort or distress ratings. And everyone experiences discomfort or distress at different levels for different things. You are the boss of this process and the good news is – it's all good!

Every step out of your comfort zone is a step to stand up to worry and fear and realign with a life that you choose, not a life that worry and fear are telling you to live. The only consideration is that it needs to bring on some level of discomfort – because if it doesn't then it's still in your comfort zone and you're not then conquering anxiety. That's the paradox of anxiety: in order to reduce anxiety, you need to allow yourself to experience the anxiety – in small amounts, of which you are the boss, so you build up resilience over time.

So map out an action plan starting with small steps, even what you might consider teeny steps, that are just out of your comfort zone. The steps you want to map out involve gradually approaching those avoided situations.

It is important to recognise that this is not about waiting until there is no fear before you approach a challenging situation. If you did this then you would end up just staying in your cosy comfort zone. Instead, reflect on whether fear is underpinning your actions and realign them with a values-driven pathway. Recognise that you are in the Anticipation Zone. That dirt mound might feel like Mount Everest at first, but the more you climb it the more you will build up evidence that worry is wrong. You can do it! You can cope much better than worry would have you believe.

Understanding that anxiety is a physiological reaction to worry thoughts and does not actually mean that there is a tiger in your midst allows you to change your relationship with the anxiety feelings. Even though the feelings are uncomfortable, you now know to no longer interpret them as something catastrophic. In doing that, you take yourself out of the fight or flight reaction and dissolve the anxiety feelings rather than exacerbate them.

It is only after approaching rather than avoiding that you can lay down new learning, conquer worry and move from anxiety to resilient and values-aligned action. Success with conquering anxiety involves actually allowing the anxiety to be there in small amounts while approaching those avoided situations. You don't want to try to push the anxiety away before approaching; you instead want to get used to the situation and let the anxiety subside in and of itself.

This is courage. It involves leaning into uncertainty and sitting with the discomfort that uncertainty brings, rather than trying to get rid of the discomfort and retreating back into certainty. It is an attitude of: 'Maybe it will and maybe it won't, but I can move forward alongside the feelings of anxiety.'

Embrace behavioural experiments

Think of yourself as a scientist. You are now engaging in behavioural experiments to test out whether your worry thoughts were the reality or whether worry was wrong. Keep in mind that worry will try to trick you into believing an inflated likelihood estimate of something bad happening, an inflated awfulness estimate of the negative outcome, and a deflated estimate of your capacity to cope in that situation. It is only through testing this out that you will discover whether worry was right or whether worry was wrong. What we know is that the likelihood of something bad happening is far lower than worry tricks us into believing, the situation is much less awful than worry tricks us into believing, and we cope much better than worry has us believing we will. As a scientist you are able to test out the theory and prove that worry is wrong.

MIND STRENGTH ACTION

Approach avoided situations

See if you can build your list of behavioural experiments now. Have a think about what you are avoiding and would love to experience if you could leave fear at the door. Write that list down now and then rate each behavioural experiment on perceived discomfort or distress. Remember, you are moving out of the Anticipation Zone into the Actual Zone and wearing

>>

down that avoidance hump over time. As you do, you will build up courage and stretch that comfort zone, creating a new, larger comfort zone.

As explained, everybody goes at their own pace and that's okay – there's no right or wrong. You might want to take things very slowly and gradually or you might want to move ahead rapidly. Either is absolutely fine. Generally, you want to stay at each stage with repeated exposure to feared situations until it becomes straightforward and, well, boring. A rough guide to when you are ready to move on to the next behavioural experiment is when your discomfort rating is at about a 20/100. Only move on to the next behavioural experiment when you feel ready – your gut feeling will guide you.

Approaching avoided situations involves the following steps:

1. Brainstorm and write down a list of avoided situations.
2. Brainstorm and write down a list of safety behaviours.
3. Rate each avoided situation on level of discomfort or distress, where 0 = no discomfort/distress and 100 = maximum discomfort/distress.
4. Engage in your behavioural experiments, approaching avoided situations while letting go of your safety behaviours, starting with the ones that trigger only mild discomfort or distress.
5. Reflect on whether the experiment supported:

Possibility A – That your worries were real (something bad will happen, it will be a catastrophe and you won't be able to cope).

Possibility B – That your anxiety just reflected a worry problem and you can stand up to worry and move forward down a values-driven path instead.

Keeping a record of your behavioural experiments is an essential tool in building up a body of evidence that worry was wrong and that even if things don't go entirely according to plan, the outcome isn't a catastrophe, and you are building resilience.

Here's a sample worry sheet you can use to record these patterns. To download this sheet and more helpful tools, visit drjodie.com.au.

SITUATION	What is worry tricking me into thinking?	What can I do to stand up to worry?	What was the outcome?	What can I learn from this?

Before you know it, you will find that you are living in much greater alignment with the life you want to live, not the life that worry, rumination and self-doubt are telling you to live. Keeping a record helps you to look at the evidence of what the outcome is compared to what worry was telling you. No matter what the outcome, helpful learning eventuates from these behavioural experiments.

Case Studies

Let's look at how avoidance played a role in Ella, Allie, Mike, Adam and Luke's lives, and the effectiveness of approaching avoided situations through behavioural experiments.

Recall Luke's fear of dogs. Avoidance was taking hold in Luke's life. He avoided any situations where there might have been a chance that a dog was there, such as at parks or beaches. He avoided going to friends' houses if they had a dog and would invite them to his house instead. He would cross the road if he saw a dog being walked up ahead. Over time his fear had increased to the point that he avoided reading books if he knew that a dog was in the story. His fear and avoidance were getting so extreme that he even felt anxious if somebody used the word 'dog' and would then think twice about leaving the house. At the time Luke first came to The Anxiety Clinic with his parents, his fear of dogs was starting to take over his life. He had fun with his friends at school and wished he could go to parties and sleepovers. He enjoyed sport but missed out on opportunities to play outdoors and kick a ball with his family.

Luke and his parents engaged in the strategies of the Mind Strength Method and he was able to overcome his fear of dogs within weeks. Once he and his parents were able to conceptualise worry as a bully bossing Luke around, they could work as a team to stand up to fear. Let's look at how Luke applied the Mind Strength Method to help him.

First of all, Luke was able to notice the worry story and put the book back on the bookshelf. Then it was time to gradually approach his avoided situations. Worry still tried to boss him around and tell him not to approach the situations but although the voice was there telling him that he needed to avoid certain situations, he accepted the voice and recognised that he didn't have to listen. He had a choice: go down the fear-driven path or to go down a values-driven path and gradually approach those avoided situations.

Luke's list of avoided situations looked like this.

MY BEHAVIOURAL EXPERIMENT LIST	Level of discomfort
Writing the word 'dog'	10
Reading and saying the word 'dog' out loud	10
Reading a children's book about a dog	15
Watching a cartoon about a dog	15
Reading a factual book about dogs	25
Watching internet videos about dogs	25
Going to the pet store and watching the puppies	40
Going to the pet store and touching a small puppy	50
Going to the pet store and touching a large puppy	70

MY BEHAVIOURAL EXPERIMENT LIST	Level of discomfort
Going to the pet store and holding a small puppy	70
Going to the pet store and holding a large puppy	80
Walking around the block without a water bottle	50
Walking around the block and passing a small dog on a leash	40
Walking around the block and passing a large dog on a leash	50
Going to a park with dogs on leashes	50
Going to a park with dogs on leashes and patting a dog	60
Visiting a friend who owns a small dog	55
Going to a friend's house and patting the small dog	60
Visiting a friend who owns a large dog	55
Going to a friend's house and patting the large dog	70
Going to a park with dogs off leashes	90
Going to a park with dogs off leashes and patting a dog	95

At first the voice of worry was loud: 'Don't do it, something disastrous will happen. A dog will be there. You never know, there's a chance that it will be ferocious. There's a chance that it will hurt you. There's a chance that it will kill you.'

When our brain is hijacked by our amygdala, we don't think in rational terms. For people with an anxiety disorder this can indeed be terrifying. Luke persisted with determination. He practised saying hello to worry. He became good at recognising the sound of worry's voice and the tricks that worry played. He recognised the fear-driven path that worry was trying to take him down. He practised the STOP Strategy (see page 154), took long, slow out-breaths, and mapped out a plan of action to take him down a values-driven path instead – a path that engaged in sporting activities, parties with friends and sleepovers at homes, regardless of whether dogs were there. The more behavioural experiments he engaged in, the more evidence he built up to demonstrate that worry was wrong and that he was able to cope.

One of Allie's main avoided situations was speaking up in class. She set herself one behavioural experiment every tutorial where she purposefully answered a question. This served a double benefit of approaching the avoided situation of speaking up in class and embracing imperfection, which she had also avoided. She practised purposeful imperfection gradually, such as saying silly things to strangers or asking for directions at the risk of looking silly. She had avoided being assertive and so engaged in behavioural experiments in which she practised speaking up for herself, such as asking to pass someone on the escalator or asking a lecturer if she didn't know something. At first this was extremely challenging, but the more she did it the easier it became.

Allie had also avoided going on dates for fear of embarrassing herself, being rejected or being judged in some negative way. Through the course of therapy, Allie began seeking out opportunities to date new people. She engaged in these as behavioural experiments, leaning into purposeful imperfection and learning that just because things didn't go perfectly it didn't mean that it was a disaster. In fact, by taking steps out of her comfort zone and treating them as behavioural experiments to stand up to worry, Allie ended up establishing a fabulous new relationship.

Mike recognised that he battled with the fear of not knowing about the future. His safety behaviours kept him trapped in the struggle of trying to know for sure that things would be okay. His behavioural experiments therefore involved approaching uncertainty and adapting to the discomfort that the experience created. Mike avoided delegating and letting go of order and control. Mike took pride in his ability to do things well and became agitated when delegation resulted in other people not completing work to the standards that he expected of himself. His behavioural experiments therefore involved slowly and gradually giving tasks to others and sitting with the discomfort of the uncertainty of the outcome.

Adam's source of avoidance was his schoolwork. His behavioural experiments involved mapping out a plan of small steps in the right direction of chipping away at daily schoolwork tasks. He and his family worked together to help Adam bring his focus back to effort and away from outcome, and to be proud of himself for effort towards his schoolwork, no matter how small. Every small step was a step in the right direction. After completing these behavioural experiments , he rewarded himself for his efforts. His rewards were built around values-aligned activities, such as doing some fun things with his school friends and family. Adam's parents also responded beautifully to therapy, ensuring that they too focused their verbal recognition on effort not outcome.

Adam's other source of avoidance was social interaction, escaping into gaming and internet addiction. Adam mapped out a plan of behavioural experiments that helped him to focus on taking steps out of his comfort zone to engage in some local social groups and sporting activities. The more he engaged in these activities, the more he learned that the outcome wasn't a catastrophe, and he built up resilience and social skills that made the interactions easier over time.

Ella's main source of avoidance was imperfection. So she built a plan to engage in situations imperfectly and sit with the discomfort that this experience created. These predominantly involved letting go of her safety behaviours of cleaning, checking and people-pleasing. For example, her behavioural experiments involved seeing if she could not turn up exactly on the minute of her appointments, or not be impeccable in her appearance, or embrace purposeful imperfection with her household.

Ultimately, Ella learned to recognise that if she experienced mild anxiety, it meant that she was taking steps out of her comfort zone and sitting with the discomfort of imperfection, rather than struggling and grappling with it in order to get rid of the anxiety and maintain the unrealistic benchmark of perfection. The more she took steps out of her comfort zone and approached being purposefully imperfect, the easier it became and the more liberated she felt. She created a series of behavioural experiments that allowed her to engage in situations imperfectly.

Through these experiments, Ella learned that engaging in behavioural experiments that triggered a mild amount of discomfort or distress was enough to help her learn that she could cope and disasters didn't happen. There were times when things didn't go exactly to plan, but these moments provided her with excellent learning and demonstrated that even if things weren't perfect, she could cope and the outcome was not a catastrophe.

On one occasion, Ella was experimenting with not attending to her emails immediately. She had undertaken a string of behavioural experiments and was pushing things very hard to achieve as much as she could as quickly as she could to get over the anxiety. She also happened to not be feeling so well on that day and noticed that the anxiety started to go into a bit of a tailspin. She found herself becoming anxious about being anxious and noticed that her mind was getting caught up in a negative worry story about her not being any good. It was at this point that Ella and I regrouped on what was going on for her and why things started to feel tricky. There was a lot of learning to be had through this particular experience.

A fundamental consideration is that even though Ella's behavioural experiments were aimed at the goal of approaching rather than avoiding imperfection, there was one form of perfectionism that was proving problematic. Ella was applying her perfectionistic standards on her engagement with therapy! As a result, her expectations of her approach to the behavioural experiments was to move through them quickly and to do them perfectly! This meant that she took on too much too soon and tipped her experience into a panic attack.

First of all, it is important to recognise that setbacks are a normal and understandable part of this journey. You are ultimately changing longstanding mental habits, and these kinds of habits are hard to break – but they are breakable. The Mind Strength Method is about neuroplasticity – changing the pathways in the brain through the purposeful reactions that you adopt in any particular moment. This is not easy and it takes courage, persistence and self-compassion.

The challenge that Ella was experiencing was that she was back in the boxing ring, struggling and fighting the anxiety when it came up, rather than noticing, observing and allowing it. When anxiety comes up, you don't want to hate it; you want to observe it, allow it and recognise that it is understandable that it is there. You want to engage in the behavioural experiments not with the intention of getting rid of the anxiety but with the intention of moving forward alongside it. As soon as you find yourself doing behavioural experiments with the intention of getting rid of the anxiety you create anxiety. This is the paradox. It is acceptance of the anxiety that liberates you from the anxiety. Just as it is the acceptance of worry that helps you to move beyond the worry and loosen its grip on you.

• • •

Although there is no right or wrong in the approach you take with your behavioural experiments, keep the analogy of getting used to the water at the beach front of mind. A stepwise approach is typically the best way to go, where you put your toe in the water first until you are ready to take another step in. I typically go into the water inch by inch – and that's okay! The beautiful thing about this is that we get used to the water, and what feels cold and unpleasant initially starts to warm up. So, if you are getting frustrated with yourself when you engage in the behavioural experiments, recognise the following:

1. If there is no anxiety, then you are still in your comfort zone.
2. If there is anxiety, this means that you are stretching your comfort zone and are on the right path.

3. You need to approach avoided situations gradually – you are the boss of you and you know the pace that works best for you: it's all good.
4. You have to be kind to yourself along the way. Standing up to worry and approaching avoided situations is hard. Focus on effort, and remember that every step you take is a learning opportunity and worthy of celebration.

Now that we have covered the first part of behavioural experiments, approaching avoided situations gradually, we will turn our attention to the second part: letting go of the behaviours that worry pushes you into in those situations. This is the second way worry tricks you. Remember the 'struggling in quicksand' behaviours that worry says you have to perform in order to stay safe? These are your safety behaviours.

Approaching avoided situations is a tremendous step forward. Letting go of your safety behaviours while engaging in these avoided situations is embracing life with mind strength – and this is true empowerment.

Chapter 20

TOOL 6

Let go of your safety behaviours

It's time to stop struggling
in quicksand

Congratulations on mapping out and implementing a plan to approach avoided situations. It is a critical step in moving from anxiety, stress, worry and fear towards empowered and resilient action. However, it is only part of the path to freedom from anxiety. The next essential tool in the Mind Strength Toolkit is to let go of your mental and physical safety behaviours, those 'struggling in quicksand' behaviours that make you feel worse rather than better. As you know, these can be subtle, so look out for them. The key to defining your safety behaviours is thinking about whether your actions are driven by the push away from perceived threat, rather than the pull towards your values.

Why do you need to ensure that you let go of your safety behaviours when you approach avoided situations? Because worry can trick you into believing that you were only okay because of the safety behaviours. Worry will say you were only okay this once because you checked or because you had your friend with you. Alternatively, worry might say you'd better check because you must have certainty and if you don't check you might miss something. Keep in mind that worry's conditions and goals are unrealistic and downright unachievable – achieving certainty when there is no certainty. Whether it's certainty about health, or certainty about safety, or certainty about judgement, or about performance, or whatever that certainty might be, worry creates standards and expectations of certainty and perfection that are unattainable. So, ultimately, you are left uncertain and trapped in anxiety, agitation or distress. This, in turn, can lead to despondence, low mood and depression.

For Luke, mental safety behaviours included worrying about whether a dog might attack him or a loved one, mapping out an escape plan for upcoming events, arguing with his thoughts, and trying to block and challenge his thoughts. These were remedied by Luke and his parents practising calling him out when worry was bossing him around, and by Luke's parents helping him to recognise when the book had come off the bookshelf, gently encouraging him to notice the worry story, close the book and put it back on the shelf. Instead of arguing with the worry thoughts, Luke practised mindfulness strategies of observing the thoughts, allowing the thoughts and just watching the thoughts come and go. When worry came up, Luke practised saying hello. By doing this, Luke no longer became anxious about being anxious.

Reassurance seeking was a physical safety behaviour for Luke. He repeatedly checked with his mum and dad to make sure that no dogs were going to be around, or that nothing bad was going to happen. Whereas previously Luke's parents would alleviate the stress and anxiety that were playing out for him in the short term by providing reassurance, they now recognised that this was only momentarily helpful and was keeping Luke trapped in his worries in the long run. Instead, Luke's parents changed the pattern of responding to Luke's requests for reassurance. They gently encouraged him to sit with the uncertainty either by suggesting that maybe worry was bossing him around or by saying maybe there would be a dog and maybe there wouldn't. The pattern of reassurance-seeking behaviour quickly diminished. Instead, Luke was exposed to the uncertainty without the desired response of getting reassurance. Worry was no longer winning and Luke was reclaiming his power.

The program of behavioural experiments that Luke's parents, in conjunction with a clinical psychologist, mapped out for him to approach avoided situations involved gradually letting go of having friends and family members with him when patting or approaching a dog. He also engaged in these situations while not holding onto a water bottle or a stick. These situations were engaged in gradually, and throughout the process Luke was in charge to determine what he felt ready to do at any time. As time progressed, Luke felt increasingly confident in his ability to engage in approaching avoided situations while letting go of his safety behaviours.

Luke kept a behavioural experiment record, which indicated the situation, what worry was tricking him into believing, what he was going to do to stand up to worry, what the outcome was and what he was able to learn from it. Each time he built up a body of evidence to demonstrate that worry was wrong. The more behavioural experiments that Luke engaged in to approach avoided situations while letting go of his safety behaviours, the more worry reduced in power until the worry story was just a faint whisper in the back of Luke's mind.

Let's turn our attention to Mike. Worry was rampant. His mind was active and the worry thoughts were loud. He checked repeatedly in his mind to make sure that nothing bad was going to happen, and tormented himself to make sure that he and others hadn't made mistakes in the past. The protective instinct was strong and he didn't want to let his family down. Mental safety behaviours included worrying and rumination, second-guessing himself, arguing with his thoughts, trying to rationalise his thoughts and trying to block his thoughts.

For Mike, building awareness and understanding of the nature of anxiety, and the struggle with uncertainty through rumination and worry as futile mental processes, proved tremendously helpful. He was able to let go of his relationship with worry once he recognised that not only did it not serve a helpful purpose but it actually undermined his progress. He, too, learned to let go of these mental processes as safety behaviours and turn his attention to problem-solving and action-planning as an alternative. Mike practised the book back on the bookshelf strategy at first to change mental habits and get some distance from rumination and the worry story.

Mike started to get better at noticing when his mind was tipping to outcome and at bringing it back to effort. He recognised that outcome-oriented thoughts were out of his control but effort was in his control. He practised bringing his attention back to his values. His deep desire to do the right thing by his family was ultimately values-driven, and he did not need fear to motivate him. Mike had to work with purposeful determination to let go of his physical safety behaviours. It was challenging for him to feel the agitation around health and financially related concerns and not check or seek reassurance. However, persistence and awareness paid off, and these habits loosened their grip over time as Mike learned that they only made his situation worse. Tipping the focus from worry to problem-solving and action-planning was a very helpful practical strategy.

Acceptance and awareness of his tendency to lash out and get defensive as fear-driven safety behaviours were also helpful. Mike realised that these behaviours were only ostracising him from his family and were completely out of line with his values. Mike practised the STOP strategy, which helped him build space between the situation and his response, and helped him to move out of anger and aggression to regain calm and values-aligned actions. Mike implemented a practical plan to reduce and eliminate his alcohol consumption as he recognised that this was an unhelpful safety behaviour. It was fear-driven in his attempt to quash big emotions. He replaced this with the more helpful alternatives of relaxation and exercise as part of an overarching wellbeing plan.

Ella had a similar journey to Mike. She, too, did not sit comfortably with letting go of order and control and staying with the discomfort of uncertainty. However, understanding anxiety and understanding worry and rumination as unhelpful mental processes was exceptionally helpful to Ella. She became good at noticing when worry was bossing her around. She noticed the 'Perfectionism' story and was able to put the book back on the shelf. She engaged in behavioural experiments where she embraced purposeful imperfection in order to learn that catastrophes did not happen just by letting go of being in perfect control. Examples included waiting progressively longer before answering emails and leaving the washing in a pile rather than cleaning it straight away.

As Ella engaged in her behavioural experiments of breaking down perfectionism, although it felt anxiety-provoking at first, she became used to it. Further to this, the satisfaction and freedom from stress that was brought about by Ella no longer having to regimentally adhere to her perfectionistic standards, in turn took her out of fight or flight, and letting go of order and control became progressively easier.

Ella remembered the pink elephant experiment and understood the unhelpful safety behaviour of blocking her thoughts. She instead changed the relationship with her thoughts and engaged with them mindfully, observing and allowing them to just come and go. She began saying hello to worry to take herself out of the struggle with the thoughts and practise mindfulness. She found this difficult at first but, in no time, the voice of worry became much quieter as she no longer perceived it as a threat.

One of the most challenging of Ella's behaviours was no longer over-checking her children at night. However, with persistence and determination, she was able to sit with the discomfort of uncertainty and stretch the times between checking. She applied a 'reasonable person's test' and asked herself what any reasonable person would do under these circumstances. This helped to guide her way and let go of the safety behaviours over time.

Experiment with letting go of safety behaviours

Think about the mental and physical safety behaviours that are getting in the way of you living your life the way you choose to, not the way worry is telling you to live it. Write them down.

Now start to bring the tools of the Mind Strength Toolkit together and practise letting go of your safety behaviours. See how many behavioural experiments you can do each day. You can go through the day and have no behavioural experiments or you can go through the day and have an abundance of behavioural experiments. See how many opportunities you can create to stand up to worry and fear. The more you do, the easier it gets over time and the more you build up resilience.

Can you be really good at noticing wins and celebrating effort? Remember that conquering anxiety is hard and all steps are worthy of celebration. Congratulations on your awesome efforts – by practising the tools of the Mind Strength Toolkit, you will build up mind strength over time and smash fear out of the park!

As Ella let go of her safety behaviours of needing to be perfect, it freed up more time for her to realign with her values-driven activities, such as going to the gym and catching up with her friends. These actions made her feel less stressed, resulting in a positive feedback loop and helping her to feel even better over time. Her relationship with her husband also improved, and she learned that worry, which was telling her that she had to be perfect in order to be okay, was wrong.

Allie, too, was able to stand up to worry and let go of the stories that were playing out in her mind. Understanding that worry served no purpose apart from leading to more worry was particularly helpful. She put the 'Negative Judgement' story back on the shelf. The most challenging chapter not to read was the one where she judged herself negatively. She needed to learn strategies to treat herself like her own best friend. The Mind Strength Tool 8, Stand Up to the Critical Voice and Conquer Impostor Syndrome (see page 243) was incredibly helpful for her in managing this negative self-judgement worry story.

Allie had to practise letting go of checking her social media to see what her friends were doing. She practised sitting with the discomfort of uncertainty, which proved difficult; however, over time this became easier as new habits and new learning took hold. She did this gradually and instead used this time to re-engage in specific social groups that were aligned with her valued activities. Like Ella, Allie had to face letting go of the need to be perfect and learn that this was not a catastrophe. Allie understood that starting small was absolutely fine, and she leaned into discomfort gradually. It was only in feeling the discomfort and doing it anyway that Allie was able to stretch her comfort zone and build resilience over time.

Adam's mental safety behaviours were worrying and second-guessing himself. His worry story was the 'I Will Fail' story. Adam was able to recognise the voice of worry and stand up to it. He learned to tip the focus from outcome to effort with his schoolwork, which helped him to feel more in control. As stress lessened, he became less inclined to procrastinate, which proved to make things gradually better over time, as the less he procrastinated the less work mounted up and the less stressed he felt. At the same time, Adam's parents set up some healthy boundaries around gaming and internet use. They also introduced him to some local social groups, which helped him to realign with values-driven social activities. This in turn lessened his dependence on social groups on the internet, which were predominantly fear-driven.

Chapter 21

Engage in mood boosters

Small is better than not at all

One of the most powerful tools in the Mind Strength Toolkit to curb anxiety and build resilience is to engage in mood boosters. Worry is at times accompanied by its close buddy, depression. Depression can feel like a menacing beast towering over us. Worry and depression like to spur each other on; they work as a synergistic team where they each increase the other's power.

When depression and clinical anxiety occur side by side, it is called comorbidity. The relationship between depression and anxiety can work in many ways. Some are described below.

- A genetic predisposition or vulnerability to either anxiety or depression.
- A biological vulnerability to either anxiety or depression where a challenging life experience can trigger or exacerbate either, or both.

- Anxiety or stress leading to depression.
- Depression leading to anxiety or stress.
- A traumatic life experience being the catalyst for either anxiety or depression, or both.

If you are experiencing difficulties with what you think might be depression, it is important to seek out help and guidance from a medical doctor and mental health professional for a clearer diagnosis and treatment recommendations. Depression can be a slippery slope, and your family doctor will typically be equipped with excellent strategies and refer you to a good clinical psychologist, psychiatrist or other mental health professional to help to turn depression problems around. The good news is there are excellent scientifically supported strategies to help. Your doctor might also consider prescribing medication alongside clinical psychological intervention.

Just as individuals can experience anxiety at all levels of severity, some of which might be classified as an anxiety disorder, a person can experience low mood at all levels of severity, some of which might be classified as depression. However, depression has certain signs and symptoms that are different from low mood alone. Some of these signs aren't commonly known, so it is a good idea to familiarise yourself with the features of depression, which can often go undetected. Early detection is helpful in turning depression around. Once depression is recognised, you can equip yourself with the skills to feel more empowered to stand up to it. Being proactive early can really help and can, in fact, save a person's life.

The signs and symptoms of depression

As with worry, you want to learn depression's tricks, what it looks like, what it sounds like and what it feels like. By doing this you can feel empowered to stand up to it. It is important to remember that feeling sad or down is a normal and understandable part of being human – we all experience these feelings and sometimes we just want to have a big, hearty cry. So what are the signs to look out for when feeling sad or down is something different – when feeling sad or down is, in fact, depression?

For a depression diagnosis to be made, individuals experience at least three signs and symptoms from the categories below. Keep in mind that we all experience some of these characteristics from time to time, and if you do it doesn't necessarily mean that you have depression. Similarly, depression can present differently in different people; not everyone who has depression will have all of these features. Look out for any changes that you, a family member or a friend might experience across the three broad categories described below.

Feelings

One of the most common features of depression is feeling sad, down or miserable for most of the time for more than two weeks. However, like anxiety, there are many faces and associated feelings to depression. I've included some examples of these feelings over the page.

- Feeling overwhelmed
- Irritability
- Guilt
- Frustration
- Reduced confidence
- Reduced happiness and positivity
- Feelings of indecision
- Disappointment
- Feeling miserable and sad.

Behaviour

There are a number of behavioural indicators of depression. Depression typically tells you to withdraw and that you are not worth it. Behaviourally, this might mean that you are

- not going out any more or as much as you used to
- withdrawing from close family and friends
- numbing difficult feelings through drugs and alcohol
- not getting the things done at work or school that you need to get done
- not engaging in activities that you would otherwise have enjoyed.

The loss of interest or pleasure in some of the things that would more typically give you a sense of joy and satisfaction is a common sign to look for in depression. This is called anhedonia.

Mike loved to interact with his children. He took an active interest in their lives. He would come home from work and read them bedtime stories with keen joy and connection. But as anxiety increased its impact on Mike and he became preoccupied with checking his finances and checking his health, so too depression crept in. Before he knew it, depression was telling Mike not to bother connecting with his children and his wife, because he would just be a burden to them. The depression told him to withdraw to his study or to stay at work for longer hours – because why would they possibly want him at home anyway?

Mike initially tried to shove these feelings down. He liked to think that he was strong and stoic. He couldn't understand why he was feeling this way. He recognised that he had so much to be thankful for, and tried to convince himself that he had no right to be feeling down. He felt guilt and shame that he was so self-absorbed. He started to think that people might even be better off without him, that he was simply a burden in their lives. The dark feelings and dark thoughts seemed to be escalating, and, alongside the anxiety, were becoming so terribly hard.

Mike believed that he had to just soldier on – he had a family and a household to look after, it was his duty to just 'man up' and deal with it. He turned to drink to numb the difficult feelings, and sometimes he just wanted to escape altogether. This was the dark cloud of depression. It had crept into Mike's world like a big, black fog hovering over him. He retreated inwards and saw no way out. This was until he enlisted help. We turned it around within a few months. If you or someone you know are experiencing the same, these problems can be remedied. Please don't suffer in silence.

You deserve to look after yourself and seek out the help you need. There is light at the end of the tunnel and you don't have to go through that tunnel alone.

• • •

Thoughts (the 'three Ps')

Worry tells you to avoid something because a disaster might happen, while depression tells you that *you* are the disaster.

Some examples of thoughts associated with the three Ps are

- *I'm a failure* (personal, permanent).
- *It's my fault* (personal).
- *Nothing good ever happens to me* (pervasive, personal).
- *I'm worthless* (personal, permanent).
- *Life's not worth living* (permanent).
- *People would be better off without me* (personal, pervasive, permanent).

Physical experiences

Like anxiety, depression can result in a brain fog, a feeling that you can't concentrate or that your memory is not so great. Sometimes it can feel like you are carrying around a literal heavy weight, walking through sludge, or that to move forward you have to climb an enormous brick wall. Sometimes it feels like a physical sickness. Of course, it is important to rule out any other physical health problems by seeing your medical doctor; however, if you are experiencing any of the following, it might be a sign that you are experiencing depression.

- A pervasive sense of fatigue.
- Feeling sick and run down.
- Headaches and muscle pain.
- An upset stomach.
- Difficulty sleeping or changes in sleep.
- Loss of appetite or an increase in appetite.
- Significant weight loss or weight gain.
- Difficulty concentrating and/or memory loss.

The lethargy spiral

The experience of depression creeping up on you is commonly the result of a downward spiral, sometimes called the depression spiral or 'lethargy spiral'.

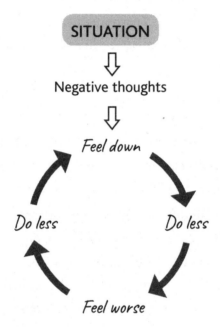

SITUATION

⇩

Negative thoughts

⇩

Feel down

Do less

Do less

Feel worse

A particular situation might trigger a flurry of unhelpful negative or worry thoughts. These negative thoughts then trigger certain emotions such as feeling down, sad or miserable. This can result in just wanting to withdraw or do less. Doing less can, in turn, make you feel worse, so you do less again and on it goes until feeling down turns into depression.

So, as a first powerful step to turning the lethargy spiral around, look out for it – answer these questions:

>>

- Is low mood starting to creep into your life?
- Are you doing fewer activities than you were a little while ago?
- Do you feel like you just want to do less or feel like you're walking through sludge?
- Do you feel more agitated, with a short fuse to anger or aggression?
- Are there things that you know you should be enjoying but you just don't feel that sense of joy?
- Do you have dark thoughts and hopelessness about the future?

If dark thoughts are taking over, please call emergency or seek urgent medical attention to get the help you need.

For a helpful toolkit to conquer fear, boost your mood and build your mind strength, go to drjodie.com.au.

Do more, strategically

So what are some of the helpful actions that you should engage in when you notice low mood starting to creep in? Central to the Mind Strength Method is recognising that all feelings are okay. It is not about not having the feelings, but rather about building self-awareness and ensuring that you respond to these difficult emotions with helpful rather than unhelpful actions.

When you are feeling down, depression will typically say, 'Don't bother, you won't be able to do it anyway.' This is the lethargy spiral in action. Instead, embrace the message that small is better than not at all. Even tiny steps to stand up to depression are better than none at all – all steps are important, worthwhile and helpful. It's these small steps that will stimulate dopamine and serotonin in your bloodstream and start to turn the lethargy spiral around. As with worry, where you feel the discomfort and do it anyway, the best way to stand up to depression is to engage in small and powerful mood boosters every day. Small and regular is the key to success.

When depression and worry are bossing you around, you sometimes need to 'fake it till you make it'. You might not feel the joy or the fun or the desire to do anything, but when you take small steps with gradual persistence and do more rather than less, you start to feel better and are ready to do more again. But when worry and depression are whispering that you are not worth it and pointing your thoughts in the direction of all the possible things that might go wrong, this is not an easy thing to do. That heavy weight is holding you down. So the key to success is to do more – strategically.

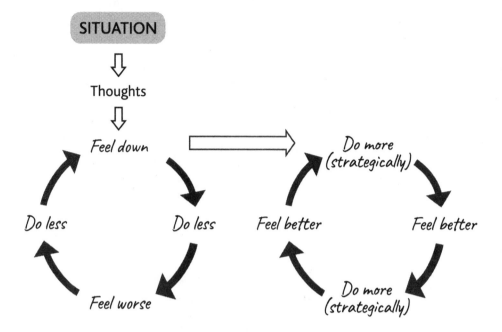

What you want to target are the things demonstrated by scientific evidence to stimulate positive neurochemicals in the bloodstream – things like serotonin, dopamine and oxytocin. These are the calming and feel-good neurochemicals that will counteract the adrenaline and cortisol and thus the actions that take place when you are feeling anxious or depressed that can typically burn up your serotonin reserves. This could be exercise; connecting with family and friends; or focusing on things that you are grateful for, no matter how small.

Remember that small and regular are what you are after. So you want to do one small thing every day from each of the areas below. And you want to do them IMPERFECTLY. More about purposeful imperfection in the next chapter.

Keep a journal

Record doing one thing from each of the scientifically supported actions below to reduce the impact of worry, curb anxiety and turn the depression spiral around. Writing things down increases commitment and holds accountability to your routine. It will also be encouraging to look back at where you began and to celebrate your effort along the way.

Acknowledge small achievements

When you're being bossed around by worry and depression, it can feel like there's a negative filter being pulled over your eyes. Worry tips your thoughts to the perceived threats and depression tips your thoughts to those perceived 'not good enoughs'. A way to stimulate positive neurochemicals and rebalance the focus is to be purposeful every day in identifying and acknowledging one small achievement, one challenge or one thing that you have mastered.

When you look out for it, you will recognise that you engage in small challenges and achievements all the time. However, the negative filter can prevent you from seeing them, and depression can pipe up and discount them. The trouble is when you don't stand up to this to acknowledge small acts of achievement, challenge or mastery, you are depriving yourself of the positive neurochemicals that you would experience if you were to acknowledge the efforts that you have undertaken. This becomes a self-sabotaging feedback loop, which contributes to the downward depression spiral.

You can go through the day and ignore these achievements or you can build accountability and recognition of them. The latter will stimulate dopamine and serotonin in your bloodstream, and counteract the neurochemicals of the fight or flight reaction.

Again, small is what matters most here. It might be acknowledging getting out of bed if you didn't feel like it, or taking a shower if depression was telling you why bother, or putting on your sports shoes despite it being hard. It might be larger things such as paying a bill, making a telephone call that you needed to make, or replying to an email. Build this accountability into your daily routine.

Taking steps out of your comfort zone is hard, and it is these daily small achievements and challenges that are worthy of purposeful recognition. So add this to your daily record – each day note down one small thing you've done that was hard. Remember to be proud of yourself for your efforts.

Exercise: take the first step

One of the most powerful tools in the Mind Strength Toolkit is increasing your activity levels. Exercise stimulates dopamine, endorphins and positive mood states. However, if you're having trouble beginning an exercise plan or following through with one, you're most definitely not alone. Even without depression or anxiety, many people struggle to get out of the sedentary habits that society has created, despite the very best of intentions. When you overlay this with worry, anxiety and depression, exercise can feel like an insurmountable challenge. While practical concerns, such as a busy schedule or feeling physically unfit, can make exercise more challenging, the biggest challenges to exercise are usually emotional.

Given the pivotal role of exercise and movement in helping to conquer both anxiety and depression, here are some practical and positive steps you can take to make exercise more fun and instinctive.

Small is better than not at all

When you hold on to the mantra 'small is better than not at all' this can make exercise easier. You don't have to spend hours in a gym to experience the physical and emotional benefits of exercise. In fact, adding just modest amounts of physical activity to your weekly routine can have a profound effect on your mental and emotional health.

I like to refer to the word 'movement' because all steps are great steps. Focusing on movement rather than exercise can help to remove the guilt, shame and fear of not being good enough that can come from any preconceived ideas about having to do the perfect gym class or the perfect run or the perfect weights session.

The first step can sometimes be taking your sports shoes out of the cupboard. Ultimately, the focus is on bringing movement into your life – inside or outside; it's all helpful. Every step that you take to stand up to worry and depression and get moving is a great one and worthy of celebration.

Make exercise heart-driven not fear-driven
As you know, the central principle of the Mind Strength Method is to be driven by values, not driven by fear. Worry can trip you up when it comes to exercise – doing exercise because you fear not being good enough. The best form of exercise and movement to do is values-driven exercise. In other words, do exercise that you enjoy and not because worry is telling you that you won't be good enough if you don't.

For example, Allie whose worry story was that other people would judge her negatively, found herself engaging in fear-driven exercise. The voice in her head would tell her: 'You should do this to lose weight' or 'You must run 10 kilometres so you can be as good as that person' or 'Unless you do those Pilates classes perfectly, you're not good enough'. Fear-driven exercise will keep you trapped. First of all, hypervigilance to threat will get you focusing in on all of your 'not good enoughs'. This is one of worry's tricks. When you engage in exercise for fear-driven reasons, you run the risk of avoiding it completely

>>

because of fear that you won't be good enough. Alternatively, you can get into a spiral of 'all or nothing' thinking and actions because the 'all' is impossible to sustain so you end up choosing the 'nothing'. Similarly, depression might tell you that you are not going to be any good at it – so why bother?

You are much more likely to stick with an exercise program that's fun and rewarding. So bring movement back to your heart and think about things that you typically enjoy doing when depression and worry are not bossing you around. Don't choose activities such as running or lifting weights at the gym just because you think that's what you should do. Instead, pick activities that fit into your lifestyle, abilities and interests, and think about how you can incorporate them into an exercise routine. Remember that this is checking in on what you value.

If the thought of going to the gym doesn't inspire you, there are many exercise alternatives. Running or walking outdoors might make all the difference. You might want to watch television as you ride a stationary bike, talk with a friend as you walk, take photographs on a scenic hike, walk the golf course instead of using a cart, or dance to music as you do household chores. Try to think about physical activity as a values-aligned lifestyle choice rather than a task to check off your to-do list.

Move mindfully

Often, exercises that have a regular rhythm such as walking, running, dancing or swimming are excellent to re-engage a calmer and more positive mood state. If you can combine these exercises with mindful engagement, where you focus your attention on the physical sensations you experience as you move, the actions can be even more effective.

Instead of zoning out or distracting yourself when you exercise, try to pay attention to your body. By really focusing in on how your body feels as you exercise – the rhythm of your breathing, the way your feet feel as they meet the ground, how your muscles flex as you move, even the way you feel on the inside – you'll become much better at observing, accepting and allowing your internal and external experiences to just be in the present moment rather than fighting them. This, in turn, will ease worry, anxiety, low mood and stress. Activities that engage both your arms and legs, such as walking, running, swimming, weight training, rock climbing, skiing and dancing, are great choices for practising mindfulness.

Be kind to yourself

Self-compassion and kindness when it comes to exercise and movement are also keys to success. Research shows that self-compassion increases the likelihood that you'll succeed in any given task. So don't beat yourself up about your body, your current fitness level, or your supposed lack of willpower. That will just demotivate you. Instead, look at every step as a great one that will build on the last in a positive way.

Focus on consistency not outcome

Tip the focus away from outcome and towards consistency. Consistency is the key to success when it comes to exercise as

>>

a powerful mood booster. Find ways to schedule exercise and movement into your daily routine so your brain can get used to anticipating it and take the thinking and guesswork out of it. Consider exercise an important appointment and mark it in your daily agenda.

Focus on one intentional act of movement every day. You can build up from there if you choose to. Something is always better than nothing. Look at your daily routine and consider ways to sneak in activity. It's okay to break things up into exercise bites through your day. Even very small activities can add up over the course of a day. So, if you're sitting on the couch, go for a quick walk to the corner of the street and back again instead. If the thought of doing 30 minutes is arduous, do 5 minutes instead.

Small hits of dopamine-inducing exercise are a magnificent way to show worry and depression who is boss. Household chores, such as cleaning, vacuuming, sweeping, mowing and weeding, are all helpful. Take the stairs instead of the elevator or escalator. Park further away from a building entrance, rather than right out front. Get off your train or bus one stop early. The extra walking adds up and it all helps as a powerful anxiety and depression buster. It's better to start with an easy exercise goal you know you can achieve. The brilliant thing is that there is no right or wrong: it's all good! As you meet each goal, you'll build self-confidence and momentum. Then you can move on to more challenging goals.

Set reminders and a routine

Reminders and routine are secrets to success when it comes to building good habits with exercise and movement. They help to bypass depression and worry, which can try to get in the way. For example, it might be sticking to a routine such as a specific time of the day, a specific place or a cue that the brain begins to associate with exercise. It helps to put the routine on autopilot, so there's nothing to think about or decide on. The great thing is that once you get going it just gets easier rather than harder, as worry and depression lose their power.

For example, it might be that

- the alarm goes off first thing in the morning and this becomes your automatic cue to go for your walk
- you leave work for the day and head straight to the gym
- you put your sports shoes right next to your bed so you're in them immediately.

Consider making exercise easy by planning your workouts for the time of day when you're most awake and energetic. If you're not a morning person, for example, don't undermine yourself by planning to exercise before work. See if you can plan ahead and remove things that might get in the way of exercising. Do you tend to run out of time in the morning? Get your workout clothes out the night before so you're ready to go as soon as you get up. Do you skip your evening workout if you go home first? Keep a gym bag in the car so you can head out straight from work.

>>

It can be helpful to commit your exercise goals to another person. If you've got a workout partner waiting, you're less likely to miss an exercise session. Or ask a friend or family member to check in on your progress. Announcing your goals to a social group, either online or in person, can also help keep you on track.

Build in rewards

It's a great idea to also build rewards into the process. People who exercise regularly tend to do so because of the rewards it brings to their lives, such as more energy, better sleep and a greater sense of emotional wellbeing. These are some wonderful longer-term rewards. When you're starting an exercise program, especially as part of an overarching mission to conquer anxiety and depression, it can be helpful to give yourself immediate rewards when you successfully complete a workout or reach a new fitness goal. Choose something you look forward to, such as having a hot bath or a favourite cup of tea. Alternatively, you can engage in rewarding activities alongside the exercise, such as listening to an audiobook or watching your favourite TV show while on a treadmill or bike.

Be creative

You can put creativity to work to make your exercise more enjoyable. Activity-based video games that are played standing up and moving around, can be a fun way to start moving. Examples might be simulating dancing, skateboarding, soccer, bowling or tennis. Once you build up your confidence, try getting away from the TV screen and playing the real thing outside. Or use a smartphone app to keep your workouts fun and interesting. Some apps are designed to immerse you in interactive stories to maintain motivation.

Combine exercise with social connection

Exercise can be a great opportunity to connect with friends. Connection is a primary mood booster, and working out with others can help to keep you motivated. For example, a tennis partner, a running club, or a water aerobics or dance class may be helpful motivators. It can be useful to harness the power of community, such as joining a soccer, basketball or volleyball team. There are many online fitness communities you can join. You can also try working out with friends either in person or remotely using fitness apps that let you track and compare your progress with each other. If you are part of a family, there are many ways to exercise together. What's more, kids learn by example. When you exercise as a family you model positive behaviour that will help your children in the future. This might include going for family walks or dancing to music while you do chores as a family.

Connect with others

Human beings have evolved from tribes and as a result we crave connection. In primitive times, being part of a tribe meant that we were stronger and more protected from predators, and that hunters and gatherers could work together to create a sustainable environment and a more certain future. We were interdependent. Connection was critical to our very survival.

Depression and worry tell us to withdraw and disconnect. Worry tells us to disconnect because something bad might happen or people might reject or judge us. Depression tells us we're not worthy of connection, so we shouldn't bother.

We need to be purposeful in standing up to the voice of both worry and depression, and take small daily steps to connect. The simple act of talking with another human being can trigger hormones that alleviate anxiety and boost mood. There is overwhelming scientific evidence to demonstrate that human connection with a family member, friend or a community group can calm and soothe the nervous system and ameliorate depression. Alongside this, the act of connecting with others provides a bounty of opportunities to stand up to worry and prove worry wrong.

So take a moment to think about the individuals or groups that you might want to connect with. What family members do you typically value having around you? What personal or work colleagues do you value having around? Who are the individuals in your circle of connections who treat you with kindness and respect? Check in on your intuition – what is it telling you? It will serve you well. Can you look on the internet for community groups or apps that make it easier to connect with like-minded individuals? Are there charity groups, exercise and movement groups, art and craft groups, music groups, movie groups or other special interest groups that you could connect with online to join events and arranged activities? Are there any opportunities offered through your local council, your neighbourhood, university or school community?

Can you experiment with choosing yes rather than choosing no? Remember that worry will tell you something bad is going to happen, and depression will tell you you're not worth it in the first place. In order to make both lose their power, allow yourself to ever so gradually approach and breathe through the feelings – the fear, the agitation or the low mood – rather than avoid them. The truth of the situation will be revealed.

1. Nothing bad happened.
2. The outcome wasn't a catastrophe.
3. We coped much better than worry and depression were tricking us into believing and we built up resilience.

Brainstorm a list of connections and see if you can make one act of connecting with someone every day, no matter how small. The key to success is to feel the unease and do it anyway. This is how you prove worry and depression wrong and build resilience. By engaging rather than avoiding, you learn that even if something isn't perfect it's not a disaster. You stimulate positive neurochemicals of serotonin, oxytocin and dopamine, and you turn the depression and worry spiral around.

Adopt an attitude of gratitude

There's a large amount of scientific research from the school of positive psychology demonstrating the magical power of gratitude to improve your mental and physical wellbeing. Gratitude rebalances the scales towards the positive. It's only fair really – it counterbalances our inherent negativity bias that is hard-wired in our brains to protect us from threatening circumstances.

No matter your life circumstances, you can always find something to be grateful for. Gratitude activates a powerful chemical reaction of feel-good neurotransmitters and hormones surging through your bloodstream, which in turn lift your mood. They help you to be more energised and focus more on the positives.

So see if you can practise seeking out the silver lining. Experiment with spending two weeks ending each day by reflecting on one to three things you are grateful for from that day and writing them down in a gratitude diary. Alternatively, you can note them down on a small piece of paper, roll them up and let them accumulate in a jar. At the end of the two weeks, reflect on the impact intentionally practising gratitude has had on your mood. If you find that it's been helpful, keep it going. Engaging in these activities has the added benefit of letting you look back on the things you've written down at those times when you can do with an extra hit of positivity. See page 287 for more on gratitude.

Embrace the outdoors

The next powerful mood booster is to get into the outdoors. We are biological beings. Humans were designed to roam in fields and pick fruit from trees. However, our contemporary society has led us to be predominantly sedentary in the indoors. Commonly, the expectation of our First World culture is to sit at desks in front of screens. We can go for many days where the closest to green we can get is the green images we see on our computer screens. This feeds into anxiety, depression and the lethargy spiral (see page 216). We withdraw from the outdoors and feel worse so we withdraw more.

It is helpful to be purposeful in standing up to this and embracing the outdoors. As with exercise and movement, engage in activity scheduling and build it into your daily routine. Remember the mantra: small is better than not at all. What is one small thing you can do each day to get outdoors? It might be going into your backyard, breathing the air and experiencing the sun or the wind on your face. It might be walking around the block or going to the park close to where you live. It might be going to the beach or anything else that aligns with some of the activities you value. Once again, the good news is that it's all good.

Instead of driving everywhere, you might consider walking or cycling when the distance is doable. Owning a dog, if it aligns with your lifestyle, can be helpful. Playing with a dog and taking it for a walk, hike or run are fun and rewarding ways to

>>

>> *Embrace the outdoors – continued*

fit outdoor activity into your schedule. Joining a community group that engages in outdoor activities can be particularly helpful both for conquering anxiety and boosting your mood. Remember that worry and depression will tell you to make all sorts of excuses not to do it – stand up to both, take small steps out of your comfort zone using the tools in the Mind Strength Toolkit, and you're on your way.

MIND STRENGTH ACTION

Do something pleasant, kind and fun

Just as it is helpful to identify activities that give you a sense of achievement, challenge and mastery, no matter how small, it is helpful to ensure that you do small activities daily that give you a sense of fun or are pleasant and kind, both for yourself and others. By engaging in simple and pleasant activities you will improve your mood, your energy levels, your confidence and your resilience. Some examples include

- planning a holiday
- buying something for yourself
- going to the beach
- drawing or painting
- rearranging or redecorating your room or house
- reading stories, novels, poems or plays
- breathing in the outdoors

- watching TV
- solving a problem, puzzle or crossword
- catching up with a friend
- taking a shower
- writing stories, novels, plays or poetry
- patting a pet
- hiking
- singing
- going to a party or social group
- playing a musical instrument
- combing or brushing your hair
- going out for lunch
- cooking
- doing craft
- taking a bath
- being with your children
- putting on makeup
- gardening
- wearing new clothes
- dancing
- sitting in the sun
- listening to the radio
- giving a gift
- going to the park
- helping someone
- writing in a diary
- painting your nails
- putting on moisturiser
- playing a board game
- swimming
- going for a run.

Consistency is key to success, so it is about small activities every day. These activities – combined with exercise, enjoying the outdoors, connecting with others and acknowledging small achievements – will turn the depression spiral around and stimulate positive neurochemicals. These, in turn, will help you to feel more empowered to move from anxiety, stress, worry and fear into resilience, mental strength and wellbeing.

For a helpful toolkit to help you conquer fear, boost your mood and build mind strength, go to drjodie.com.au.

Let go of 'all or nothing' thinking

There can be a tendency when you're feeling anxious or depressed to engage in 'all or nothing' thinking, also known as 'black and white' thinking. This refers to thinking of things in extreme terms. You might place perfectionistic expectations on yourself or others and be highly critical if those standards are not achieved. Alternatively, you might think in extremes such as a belief that

- you will fail the exam
- you won't ever find a partner
- you made a complete idiot of yourself at the party
- you're completely worthless.

These are the sorts of thoughts that can take hold when worry, rumination or depression are bossing you around. All or nothing thinking is hardly ever helpful. It is rare that an individual is all good or all bad – most of the time we are somewhere in between. It is far more realistic and helpful to start to think of yourself and others in non black and white terms and instead to seek out the colours in between.

These steps can help with this.

1. Notice when all or nothing thinking is happening.
2. Label the kind of thought as all or nothing thinking rather than getting hooked in to the content of the thought.
3. Gently tip the focus away from the unhelpful thought.
4. Focus instead on a values-driven alternative.

Celebrate effort

When you have a big nasty bully whispering in your ear telling you that you are not worth it and why bother because it's only going to turn out badly anyway, you need to focus on effort and celebrate every step you take. Every step is a big achievement and absolutely worthy of celebration. Remember that worry will make you focus on outcome in its attempt to gain certainty. This is coupled with the inherent negativity bias that will kick in and tell you that something bad will happen so don't do it. When depression is bossing you around, this inherent negativity bias is supercharged – it behaves like it is on steroids. So being purposeful in tipping the focus back to effort, and celebrating effort, is an essential tool in your Mind Strength Toolkit.

So what does celebration look like? It is quite simply acknowledging effort, no matter how small, and giving yourself a pat on the back for that effort. This will stimulate positive neurochemicals and start to break down the power that worry and depression can have over you.

1. Notice when your mind is focused on outcome.
2. Bring the focus back to effort.
3. Be proud of yourself for that effort – no matter how small.

Personify depression

Get to know the voice of depression and the tricks it plays. Just as you can for worry, you can personify it, learn its tricks and learn that, ultimately, it's just an unhelpful and mean story that's playing out in your mind. You have a choice of whether to listen to the voice of depression or to stand up to it. You can learn to notice it, observe it, say hello to it, and pivot and respond with helpful rather than unhelpful actions.

Managing stress and burnout

As you now know, stress can be positive, keeping you alert, focused, motivated, energised and ready to avoid danger (see page 45). However, the stress response can become negative if faced with continuous challenges without relief. When the stress response is chronically activated it can cause both physical and emotional wear and tear. Under these circumstances, you might feel frazzled, overloaded and exhausted. If you don't see any hope of a positive shift in your situation, stress can turn into burnout, which is a recognised precursor to mood and anxiety disorders (see page 71). Depression and burnout can feel similar to each other, and can be remedied in similar ways. If you suspect that you are experiencing burnout, engaging in the strategies covered in this chapter will be helpful.

Although sometimes the context might feel like no matter how hard you work, nothing is making a difference, take comfort in knowing that practising the strategies of the Mind Strength Method for curbing anxiety, conquering worry and building resilience is critical for both mitigating and remedying stress and burnout. For example, identifying what's in your control and what's out of your control will help you to alleviate some of the mental load. Recognise that you can only change what's in your control in the first place. Of the things that are in your control, tip the focus from worry to problem solving and action-planning. Focus on effort not outcome – and, once again, be proud of yourself for making the effort!

Moving from a focus on perceived threat to a focus on values is a key component in mitigating the risk of prolonged stress and burnout. The driving principle is to reflect on the reasons why you are doing what you are doing. Is it because you fear being judged negatively or you fear making a mistake? If so, embrace the strategies contained in the Mind Strength Toolkit and stand up to fear-driven actions. Your heart is filled with wisdom, so try to use your values rather than fear to determine what's important to you. Connecting with activities that are personally meaningful to you will stimulate positive neurochemicals and are surefire burnout busters.

Connecting with friends and family and engaging in values-aligned activities will melt away stress. And, while you're at it, consider sharing your stress with someone you feel close to. After all, as you know, bottling things up is a flight behaviour, and a slippery slope to more unhelpful behaviours to numb big emotions. Practising self-compassion and self-care is a far more helpful alternative. If you find it hard to lean into self-compassion and self-care, recognise that 'putting on your own oxygen mask first' means you will have much more energy and strength to help others. Socialising outside your professional group, building new friendships, finding opportunities to relax and recharge in nature, and engaging in new interests can help, too. These actions will not only help to remedy burnout, they will also provide wonderful protective benefits for future tough times. And always keep in mind the key message: small is better than not at all.

The Mind Strength Wellbeing Pyramid, covered in Chapter 24, will provide a compilation of strategies to respect the mind–body connection and further bolster you against stress, anxiety, depression and burnout. These include aspects such as good sleep habits, healthy eating, meditation and relaxation.

Burnout can also be triggered by a difficulty standing up for yourself. When we are fear driven, we can tip into being passive and feel that we have to be perfect in order to be okay. It can be easy to get caught in a pattern of saying yes to everything, which might seem easier in the short term but can keep you trapped and undermine your mental health and wellbeing in the long term. It can be a primary contributor to burnout.

———

In the following chapter you will learn about imposter syndrome and fear of failure, which can often impede our ability to embrace assertive communication and bolster us against burnout, anxiety and low mood. We will go through strategies to practise delegation, to learn how to get your needs met assertively, to practise letting go of trying to be perfect and to set more stringent boundaries. In doing so you will further conquer worry, stand up to depression and help to remedy anxiety, stress and burnout.

Chapter 22

TOOL 8

Stand up to the critical voice and conquer imposter syndrome

Can you experiment with being purposefully imperfect?

Some of our most pressing fears are the fear of being judged negatively, the fear of rejection and the fear of failure. The pervasive impact of social media results in a society where we feel compelled to present airbrushed versions of ourselves. No longer is it just the supermodels on the covers of magazines who provide an unrealistic representation of 'good enough'. Now your friends, family and neighbours present their perfect selves on social media, perpetuating a myth of needing to be perfect in order to be okay. The result is a sense of 'compare and despair'. This is coupled with a barrage of images on social media displaying the social lives and interpersonal experiences of others, which can result in anxiety or agitation driven by a fear of missing out.

As a result, social and performance anxiety are rampant. We engage in a plethora of safety behaviours to eliminate the uncertainty built around a fear of not being good enough. Checking, comparing, seeking reassurance, avoiding, worrying, ruminating, second-guessing and judging ourselves and others are just a few mental and physical safety behaviours driven by the fear of not being good enough, the fear of rejection and the fear of failure.

The ultimate representation of this challenge with uncertainty is perfectionism. Perfectionism is built on a belief that you have to be perfect in order to be okay. However, the catch with this is that there is no such thing as perfect. So, while you are trying really hard to get the perfect outcome, because there is no such thing as perfect you end up fighting a battle that can never be won.

The challenge lies in the unrealistic targets that are set – built around the myth of perfection. These unrealistic targets result in never allowing ourselves to feel good enough – we are always striving for more. Once again, what we are trying to achieve is certainty. Certainty that we won't be rejected, certainty that we won't miss out, certainty that we won't be judged, certainty that we won't embarrass ourselves and certainty that we won't fail.

When you believe that you need to be perfect in order to be okay, worry is likely to tell you that mistakes are a catastrophe and that you won't be able to cope with the consequences. As a result, when you listen to what worry is telling you, you try to be absolutely perfect because you know that if you are perfect then there won't be a catastrophe and you'll be 'safe'. So safety behaviours evolve, such as checking your work over and over again, seeking reassurance from your loved ones repeatedly, staying quiet for fear of embarrassing yourself, and working extraordinarily long hours to ensure that your work is 'perfect'.

Further to this, if you fear being judged negatively or fear failure, hypervigilance to threat is going to kick in, so you end up focusing on all your 'not good enoughs' and any slight imperfections. Your mind tips to outcome and you fail to give yourself a pat on the back for a good effort.

If your benchmark for good enough is 'perfection' and there is no such thing as perfection, you will never appear good enough in your own eyes. The result of all of these experiences is that you can end up feeling like a fraud, like an imposter – and fall victim to an increasingly recognised phenomenon known as imposter syndrome.

Imposter syndrome was rampant in both Ella and Allie's lives. Both experienced success, academically, professionally and personally, yet each felt as if they were a fraud and not actually any good. They feared that unless they remained hypervigilant through over-checking, reassurance seeking and working outrageously hard, somebody would discover that they were, in fact, 'not good enough'.

Ella and Allie's bully was a distinct kind of bully: the critical voice. This critical voice wreaked havoc in their lives. Their internal dialogue perpetually focused on their 'not good enoughs'. This was hypervigilance to threat at its core – the mind seeking out threats and focusing in on even minuscule representations of mistakes or perceived negative judgements, thereby reinforcing their stories that they weren't good enough.

Both Ella and Allie became skilled at identifying when the critical voice was bossing them around. They noticed when the 'You're a Fraud' or the 'You will Fail' or the 'You're Not Good Enough' stories came off the shelf, and learned to gently and compassionately close the book and put it back on the shelf. They also became well practised at learning when fear-driven safety behaviours, such as second-guessing and reassurance seeking, were taking hold.

MIND STRENGTH ACTION

Be purposefully imperfect

The belief that you need to be perfect in order to be okay keeps you trapped in imposter syndrome. The best way to break this unhelpful cycle is by engaging in behavioural experiments to practise being purposefully imperfect with little acts of imperfection – small inconsequential things in your day-to-day life.

By doing this, you allow yourself to learn that the outcome wasn't a catastrophe and that you coped much better than worry was tricking you into believing you would. Experimenting with imperfection might mean doing something small and silly on purpose, such as asking for directions to the train station while you are standing in front of the train station.

Keep in mind that these sorts of experiments are not about not 'stuffing up', but about confronting worry head on and demonstrating that the outcome wasn't nearly as much of a catastrophe as worry was tricking you into believing it would be. Similarly, if you have a fear of being judged negatively, for, let's say, blushing or stammering, or saying something silly, you might purposefully put blush makeup on your cheeks or stammer your words, or say or do something silly.

This can be liberating. It is only by standing up to worry and approaching these feared and avoided situations that you learn that, in telling you that the outcome would be a catastrophe, worry was feeding you garbage. The outcome wasn't nearly as bad. The other powerful element to this is that you build up resilience – you learn to cope. In fact, you end up coping much better than worry has led you to believe you would, and you tackle imposter syndrome head on.

So what are the specific fears holding you back? Use these to guide you as to the specific nature of behavioural experiments to engage in. Remember, if it is making you feel uncomfortable it means that you are out of your comfort zone, which means you are well and truly on track. In order to get over your anxiety you can't bypass it – you have to go through it, sit with the discomfort and learn that you can do it.

Practise assertive communication

A further way to stand up to imposter syndrome is by practising assertive communication. Assertiveness is your fundamental human right. It is standing up for your own needs while considering the needs of others. Assertiveness will help you align with a values-driven pathway and is empowerment at its best.

The challenge, however, is that assertive communication does not come naturally or easily to human beings, especially if you experience a fear of being judged in a negative way or a fear of failure. Fear-driven communication styles commonly fall into the categories of either being passive (the flight) or aggressive (the fight). Assertiveness is out of alignment with these primitive survival instincts, which is why humans typically find it challenging.

Passivity is a safety behaviour typically brought about by fear of not doing the right thing by somebody else, the fear of making a mistake or the fear of being judged negatively. It can be underpinned by a low sense of self-worth, where the critical voice says that you are not worth standing up for. Being passive is letting other people push their needs without consideration of your own. Alternatively, being aggressive is where individuals push their own needs without consideration of others. In contrast, assertiveness is striving for the win–win. It is standing up for your own needs while also considering the needs of others.

The good news is that assertive communication can be learned. And the more you practise, the more you are laying down new neural pathways that make assertiveness easier over time. Remember: if it feels uncomfortable, it means that you are taking steps out of your comfort zone – which is a good thing!

Think about situations you avoid despite your heart telling you that you'd love to approach them; when you shy away from getting your needs met, or when you second-guess yourself because you fear being judged negatively. These are the situations for slowly and gradually taking steps out of your comfort zone to embrace assertiveness. Remember that anticipation is the hardest part, so when you stand up to anticipation, feel the fear and do it anyway, the outcome allows you to learn that worry was wrong.

Start with those situations that produce a 30/100 in discomfort and go for it! Once again, small is so much better than not at all, and when you get going there will be no end of opportunity. For example, it might be taking an item back to a shop that you need to return, or asking to pass someone on an escalator, or asking for directions.

Here are the steps to mastering assertive communication:

1. Awareness of when your communication style is being driven by fight (aggressive) or flight (passive).
2. Awareness of assertiveness as an emotionally intelligent alternative (see page 53 for more on emotional intelligence).
3. Embrace mind strength tools to take yourself out of fight or flight.

>>

>> *Practise assertive communication – continued*

4. Move forward embracing assertive communication strategies.

A useful strategy to practise and embrace assertive communication is to follow the assertive communication formula of: 'I feel x when you do/say/are y and I would appreciate/be grateful if you could do/say/be z in the future.'

If you are used to people-pleasing, this can be a values-aligned alternative. This assertive communication strategy helps to make the person you are communicating with engage in the situation with greater empathy – it helps the other person to view the situation from your perspective. It also helps you to state your needs in a way that makes it difficult for the other person to engage defensively.

For each of your behavioural experiments, use the record sheet and hop onto the website drjodie.com.au for more tools and techniques.

Case Study

Ella practised using the assertive communication technique in both her work and home context. For example, instead of allowing worry to take hold and tell her that she had to do everything around the house, she embraced assertive communication by saying to her partner and children: 'I feel appreciated when you help me with the home chores, and I would be grateful if we could continue to do this together in the future.'

Move from outcome to effort

A final tip to break the shackles of imposter syndrome is to notice when worry is tipping you into focusing on outcome and bring the focus back to effort. For example, you might have a presentation to prepare at work and worry is getting you to focus on the outcome. Remember that this is worry's trick to get you to struggle with uncertainty and to try to find certainty when there is none. Worry and the critical voice will collude in these situations. Worry will get you struggling with finding certainty ('Will I remember what I need to say? Will I speak clearly? Will they like what I have to say?') and the critical voice will tell you that you won't be any good! You can end up facing procrastination brick walls (see page 102) for fear of failure in the midst of perfectionistic expectations.

Break down those brick walls and imposter syndrome by

- noticing when your mind is focusing on outcome
- bringing the focus back to effort
- being proud of yourself for that effort.

Ensure that you allow yourself the kindness and compassion to recognise and reward yourself when you put in effort, even if the outcome wasn't that good. When your self-worth is contingent on values-aligned effort in the present moment, you reclaim your power and stand up to imposter syndrome.

The power of internal validation

Check in on your internal voice. See if the critical voice is bossing you around, and instead try to treat yourself in the same way as you would your own best friend. This is internal validation – treating yourself with compassion and kindness. As I often remind my children, 'Who is the most important person to love? That's right – yourselves.' This is of critical importance. You go with you wherever you go, so if you can be your own best friend, that's one of the greatest superpowers you have. The ultimate representation of being your own best friend is realigning your actions to your values, focusing on effort and being proud of yourself for that effort.

Reassurance seeking is another trick of the critical voice. A fear of being judged negatively or a fear of failure commonly results in a strong need for external validation. External validation is somebody else telling you that you've done a good job, or that you look good, or that you're going to be okay. We all like being told that we have done something well; it would be rare to find someone who doesn't like that. However, you want external validation to be a 'nice to have' not a 'need to have'.

This desire for certainty based on somebody else's evaluation of yourself serves as a safety behaviour. The critical voice says that you are no good and that you had better seek reassurance to make sure you are okay. The challenge is that you only end up feeling good enough because somebody else has told you that you are good enough. As a result, when you are needy of external validation, you are giving away your power. You will feel good when you get the external validation but you will feel terrible if you don't. The byproduct of this is the temptation to engage in all sorts of people-pleasing activities in order to get validation from others. Like any safety behaviour, this might make you feel good in the short term, but then the doubt creeps back in and you feel uncertain again, keeping you trapped in this endless feedback loop of needing approval from others. Ultimately, you don't want to be driven by a need for acceptance or validation, you want companionship, friendship and connection that are aligned with your values.

Be your own best friend

A good exercise to practise is thinking about the last time a close friend or family member you care about shared something that hadn't gone well for them or a dilemma or challenge they were facing. How did you respond? Did you say kind things? Did you try to help? Write a letter, noting down the situation and the kinds of things that you said to your friend.

Now think about the last time you experienced something that didn't go very well. Write down some of the things you said to yourself in that situation. Was the critical voice on the attack? What are some of the differences that you notice between the way you spoke to your friend and the way you speak to yourself? Now practise writing that same letter to yourself in much the same way as you would speak to your close friend. Notice the tone and the words. How much better does that feel?

Sometimes, when we actually reflect on the way we speak to ourselves compared to the way we speak to others, it can almost feel like verbal abuse. I would imagine you'd never dream of talking to others with an abusive, denigrating tone – so why make it acceptable to talk to yourself that way?

See if you can incorporate a self-compassion exercise into every day. If you can provide validation, compassion and kindness to yourself, then your cup will always be full, and external validation turns from being a 'need to have' to being a 'nice to have'.

Step 3 Summary

Congratulations! You have now done the following:

1. identified your worry stories
2. identified unhelpful coping strategies
3. become aware of your heart-driven values
4. learned effective strategies to turn anxiety into action.

Now let's move to the final step.

STEP

4

Move forward
aligned with your
values and purpose

Chapter 23

Notice, pivot and adapt

Awareness and purposeful
action are the keys to success

Congratulations on coming this far. You've built awareness of your fear-driven thoughts, feelings and actions, you've built awareness of your values, you've adopted a Mind Strength Toolkit to stand up to fear, and now you are ready to power on in life and move forward aligned with your purpose and values.

Step 4 of the Mind Strength Method is about bringing all the pieces together in a values-driven action plan. In order to move from anxiety to resilient action and build mind strength, you want to establish clarity for the path ahead. Your values-driven action plan is an overarching plan combining awareness of your values with purposeful values-aligned action. Over the years, your circumstances, priorities, goals and dreams will change and that's okay. However, clarity on your desired direction facilitates empowered and purposeful action.

VALUES PYRAMID

Your plan maps out the three tiers of your Values Pyramid

YOUR HOW
Goal-driven actions

YOUR WHAT
Values-driven goals

YOUR WHY
Values and purpose

Your 'why': values and purpose

What are your values?

Refer to your comprehensive list of values on page 133. Your values provide the foundations for your most important priorities. They are your heart-driven motivations that pull you towards a life of meaning.

It becomes much easier to stand up to the voice and experiences of worry, fear, anxiety and stress when you have a clear alternative pathway. Your values are like guideposts marking out this direction – a direction that you choose to follow, not one that worry chooses. We can conceptualise your values as like your heartbeat, providing oxygen to propel you through a fulfilled life ahead.

When looking at your values list, review specifically the column identifying those values of high importance. Can you narrow your values down to around five or six of the most important? Is there one overarching value that is the most important to you? Use these as a guide for tailoring your values-aligned action plan.

What is your purpose?

Your personal purpose is what is important to you and what you want to focus on. So how do you define this purpose? With your top values front of mind, ask yourself the following five questions:

1. What are my most important values?
2. What are my past successes and times of fulfilment?
3. What are my past, present and future contributions?
4. What are my interests and passions?
5. What are my strengths, talents and skills?

Now it's time to define what is most important to you for your future purpose. Take time to consider broader areas of inspiration, such as the world around you, your family, your work, your friends and your community.

Past successes and times of fulfilment

When things have been going well in the past, or you have felt your best, most resilient and empowered self, what were the circumstances? These experiences might have been with family, at work, at school, at university, with friends, in a community group, at home, or some other circumstance. What was going on for you? Try to think of any number of these. Were there any common themes?

Past, present and future contributions

Make a list of the ways you have made a difference in the past and the things you can do to make a difference in the future. How could you contribute to the world, your family, your friends, your organisation, a future organisation, your local community, your local natural environment?

Your interests and passions

Given clarity on your most important values, note down your interests and passions. Brainstorm and write down what you discover. Often when you take thoughts out of your head and note them down, you experience a clarity you didn't have before.

Your strengths, talents and skills

Reflect on your strengths, talents and skills. What are the things you are good at that align with the things you value? Remember that being good at something doesn't mean that you value the activity or that you're interested in doing it. Satisfaction comes from aligning your strengths, talents and skills with things that you value and are passionate about. Feel free to ask trusted family, friends and colleagues what they see in you. Checking with people who you care about and who know you well is a great way to get more insights and information. (This is different from fear-driven checking due to second-guessing yourself or a need for reassurance. Rather, this is checking in for clarity and establishing more information.)

Your purpose statement

Compile your answers about these areas of personal reflection in a few paragraphs. Use this as a wonderful opportunity to embrace purposeful imperfection. This is not about having the perfect purpose statement. This is about creating a little more clarity on what satisfies you, and bringing to front of mind the areas that are important to you. Keep it short. Try writing down only a few words or phrases that describe you and your purpose. Use these words as inspiration and be true to yourself.

You might discover that the areas you feel passionate about change over time. This is completely natural. The key is to make sure you're focusing on the right purpose and passions for you. You will be your most satisfied self when you move forward in life aligned with your values and purpose. It is about taking the time to self-reflect and truly consider what energises you. Embrace clarity in the now – focus on effort rather than whether or not you have got it right. Each person's values, passions and purpose are unique to them. Nobody can tell you what yours are, and once you have greater clarity, worry had better watch out! This is the time where worry and the critical voice might try to boss you around and question your value and your worth. Use it as a behavioural experiment to notice, put that book back on the shelf and realign with the task at hand. Use your Mind Strength Toolkit to feel empowered – you know exactly what to do.

It can be helpful to ask yourself what I call the Magic Wand Question: If you could release the shackles of fear and do or be anything, what would that look like? Be inspired to think big. Be inspired to throw caution to the wind. This is a brainstorming exercise to reflect on any areas that align with what you feel most passionate about. Stand up to worry and be guided by what's in your heart.

Some key tips from the Mind Strength Toolkit for this exercise are from Mind Strength Tool 8, Stand up to the Critical

---

MIND STRENGTH ACTION

Define your purpose

Reflect on the following questions, then define your purpose statement.

1. What are your most important values?

2. What are your past successes and times of fulfilment?

3. What are your past, present and future contributions?

4. What are your interests and passions?

5. What are your strengths, talents and skills?

6. Now, write a purpose statement reflecting on the world around you, your family, your work, your friends and your community.

Voice and Conquer Imposter Syndrome. These are focusing on 'precision not perfection' and 'effort not outcome'. All ideas are worthy of getting out of your head and being captured in writing. It is not about getting it perfect and getting it right; it is about getting it down and building greater clarity for the road ahead.

Case Study When Mike undertook this exercise, the following areas provided a sense of heart-driven purpose.

The world: to help organisations to manage change and to help employees to achieve their greatest success.

My family: to be a loving and dedicated father and husband; to be a fun and optimistic role model for my children.

My organisation: to be a strong leader and a dedicated and skilled consultant for my clients. To build high productivity and motivation within my team.

My friends: to be a trusted and loyal friend and a go-to when others need a shoulder to lean on.

My community: to be an active participant in community activities and be aware and involved in social and charitable needs.

Your 'what': values-aligned goals

In order to move from anxiety to resilient action and build mind strength, you now want to identify your values-aligned goals. This involves focusing in on those values that are high on importance and low on alignment. For those values that are low on alignment, what goals would you want to achieve to bring your life into greater alignment? It is helpful if goals are solution-focused and phrased in the positive. Focus on what you want to move towards, not what you want to move away from.

Think about defining SMART goals to help to ground your ideas. The SMART acronym stands for

- Specific
- Measurable
- Achievable
- Realistic
- Time-framed

Defining SMART goals helps you to ensure that your values-driven action plan is aligned with clear points of focus and concrete action items that are within your control.

Your 'how': goal-driven actions

Once you have determined these goals, you are ready to define a goal-driven action plan to help you to get there. Build each goal with a specific plan. Focus on areas in your control and get started. Now you are ready to move forward in a values-driven direction.

Chapter 24

A life of fulfilment, resilience and wellbeing

Pulling it all together:
The Mind Strength Wellbeing Pyramid

An essential part of moving forward aligned with your values, and conquering worry, anxiety, stress and fear, is respecting the mind–body connection. An overwhelming amount of scientific research says that when you do good for your body, you will do good for your mind.

The final step in the Mind Strength Method is to map out a wellbeing plan. When you engage in an overarching wellbeing plan, you stimulate neurochemicals such as dopamine, oxytocin and serotonin, which are responsible for positive mood states and play a part in inhibiting the fight or flight reaction.

The Mind Strength Wellbeing Pyramid is built out of the core principles of positive psychology, clinical psychology, neuroscience, and scientific research on the determinants of positive mood states, mental health, wellbeing and resilience.

MIND STRENGTH WELLBEING PYRAMID

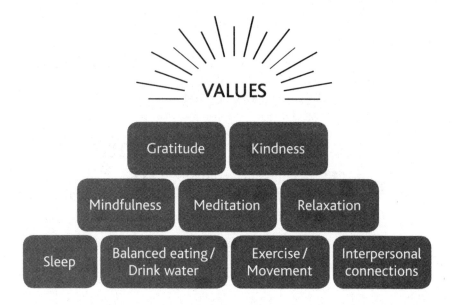

The foundation stones of the Mind Strength Wellbeing Pyramid are sleep, balanced eating, staying hydrated, exercise and interpersonal connections.

Prioritise good sleep

Prioritising good sleep is one of the foundation stones of mental health and conquering anxiety. The evidence demonstrates a clear link between sleep problems and mental health difficulties, such as stress, anxiety and low mood. This relationship is bidirectional, where poor sleep contributes to heightened anxiety, stress and depression, and these in turn contribute to poor sleep.

Whether you're having trouble falling asleep or staying asleep, there are plenty of ways to improve your sleep so you feel less stressed, more productive and emotionally resilient. I often start by helping people to notice worry and then to get some distance from the thoughts or the worry story, which might specifically be the 'You Won't Get to Sleep' story. This sets up a mental struggle where you start to try really hard to prove worry wrong: your brain gets hooked into the fight or flight reaction and you fight and struggle with the fact that you are not falling asleep.

This then keeps your brain in fight or flight, which releases adrenaline and cortisol into your bloodstream – the opposite neurochemicals from those needed to fall asleep! Remember the tiger? The last thing you want to do if you are being chased by a tiger is to fall asleep or fall in love, so when you are in fight or flight your oxytocin and melatonin shut down.

Case Study Sleep was a challenge for Ella when she first came to the clinic. She was having a great deal of difficulty both with sleep onset and disrupted sleep. Her mind was racing every time she put her head on her pillow and sometimes she would wake up in a state of panic. Despite being exhausted, Ella felt that she simply could not quieten the thoughts in her head. These weren't just overt worry thoughts; these were thoughts about productivity, action-planning and anything and everything. The common themes underpinning this mental flurry were the 'I'm Not Being Good Enough' story and the 'Perfection' story.

MIND STRENGTH ACTION

Mindfulness for sleep

Mindfulness is a great tool for when you're struggling with falling asleep. You want to notice when worry thoughts are trying to hook you in, then get some distance from that story. You then want to re-engage in the present moment and slow your breathing down. This takes you out of the fight or flight and helps you to fall asleep. When this is done in combination with lifestyle strategies involving good exercise and movement, relaxation, a reduction in caffeine and healthy balanced eating, acceptance of not falling asleep will take you out of the fight or flight reaction. When you take yourself out of the fight or flight reaction with sleep, neurochemicals for sleep onset, such as melatonin, are released into the bloodstream, increasing your likelihood of falling asleep.

Ella hated the thoughts coming up when she just wanted to go to sleep. As a result, she struggled and battled and tossed and turned to try to fall asleep. She was determined to find the perfect remedy. She tried natural remedies, food remedies, drink remedies, relaxation remedies, darkness remedies, counting remedies and technology remedies. She sought specialists and started to think that maybe she actually had a medical problem that was getting in the way of sleeping. She searched the internet for medical problems that affect sleep and sought medical advice, which sent her along another tangent of suggested remedies.

The fundamental and overarching problem was that all of Ella's struggling to fall asleep kept her brain stimulating the neurochemicals that were designed for the primary purpose of keeping a person awake! Ella and I worked through the neuroscience of the fight or flight reaction and helped her to recognise that all her attempts to fall asleep were actually serving as safety behaviours. They had the opposite effect of their intended purpose: the struggle to fall asleep was keeping her awake. Ella did not have a sleep problem – she had a worry problem.

As a result, we reviewed all the things that Ella was doing to try to fall asleep and scaled back. Ultimately, the key to success is counterintuitive – acceptance of not falling asleep is actually the key to falling asleep.

Ella turned her perspective on sleep around completely and before she knew it her sleep was restored. When the worry story about fear of not falling asleep came up, she retrained her brain to sit with the discomfort of uncertainty, which ensured that she did not slip back into the fight or flight struggle with sleep – instead she noticed the worry story, said 'maybe I will and maybe I won't', and embraced mindfulness strategies to sit with her breath in the present moment. There were, of course, times when she didn't fall asleep easily; however, she understood the rationale of acceptance, engaged in mindful breathing strategies, sat with the uncertainty as to whether or not she would fall asleep and then floated off into slumber.

Eat a balanced diet

While an accredited practising dietician is best qualified to give specific guidance regarding supplements and diet recommendations, there is an abundance of evidence to demonstrate that eating food that's better for you can assist with improving

- your mood
- your overall sense of wellbeing
- your capacity to manage stressful life experiences
- your ability to manage anxiety.

Eating a diet filled with processed foods, refined carbohydrates and sugary snacks can worsen symptoms of anxiety and stress. Sugar is absorbed quickly into the bloodstream, and this rapid absorption causes a glucose spike and an initial surge of energy. The challenge is that the energy surge wears off quickly as the body increases insulin production to eliminate the sugar from the bloodstream. This can result in a post-sugar slump and fatigue, which can detrimentally impact mood and contribute to symptoms of anxiety. If this forms a repeated cycle, it can result in ongoing fluctuating energy levels and mood states, making you more susceptible to irritability, stress, a sense of loss of control, and exacerbated anxiety.

Research suggests that foods containing vitamins and minerals such as folate, choline, vitamin B12, vitamin E, vitamin C, magnesium and zinc are helpful in reducing the symptoms of anxiety. Similarly, evidence supports the benefits of omega-3 fatty acids (EPA and DHA) and the amino acid tryptophan, a precursor of serotonin. This translates to a diet rich in fresh fruits and vegetables, leafy greens, wholegrains, dairy, lean meat and poultry, legumes, nuts, seeds, healthy oils and oily fish such as salmon, tuna, trout, mackerel and sardines. These foods help to regulate blood glucose levels, which in turn keep mood regulated. For example, wholegrains take longer for the body to break down, and release sugar into the bloodstream slowly. Similarly, eating protein at breakfast will assist in starting the day with sustained energy and more stable blood glucose levels, helping to regulate mood and mitigating susceptibility to anxiety and stress.

There is also emerging evidence to support the impact of the microbiome–gut–brain axis, or psychobiotics, on anxiety and mood. What you eat can change the composition and metabolic activity of the gut microbiota. A diet that is high in prebiotics, or fermentable fibres (e.g. vegetables, fruit and wholegrains), as well as probiotics, or fermented foods (e.g. yoghurt, sauerkraut, kimchi, tempeh and kefir) is believed to prevent neurotoxicity through anti-inflammatory and antioxidant effects, and reduce susceptibility to stress and anxiety.

Stay hydrated

Staying hydrated can impact our overall sense of mental health and wellbeing. Even mild dehydration can detrimentally impact mood, stress, anxiety and irritability. Sipping water throughout the day is the protection against dehydration that you need.

When hydrating, choose drinks wisely. The caffeine in tea, coffee, cola and energy drinks is a stimulant, which might increase susceptibility to anxiety in some individuals, so it should be consumed in moderation. Coffee is also known to inhibit levels of serotonin in the brain. When serotonin levels are suppressed, it can detrimentally impact your mood and increase irritability. Caffeine also stays in the system for many hours. If consumed in the late afternoon or evening, it may contribute to difficulty falling asleep or staying asleep.

Similarly, be cautious of alcohol consumption. Alcohol is a depressant. Heavy drinking may contribute to mood dysregulation, may inhibit medication effectiveness and can impact your quality of sleep.

While fruit juices might seem to be a positive alternative, without the fibre of whole fruit you just end up drinking nutritious sugar water that has the same rollercoaster impact of a sugar lift then slump. Sugar-free drinks might seem like another helpful alternative, but the artificial sweeteners they often contain can also have a negative impact on mood and anxiety. So limit or avoid alcohol, caffeine, fruit juice and artificial beverages. Drinking water throughout the day is an important foundation stone for wellbeing.

Find exercise you enjoy

Exercise is a powerfully positive contributor to moving from anxiety to effective action. Research demonstrates that even just 5 minutes of aerobic exercise in your routine can be helpful to reduce the impacts of anxiety. Doing a focused activity can also help you feel a sense of accomplishment.

Increasing your heart rate changes the brain's neurochemistry, increasing the availability of anti-anxiety neurochemicals such as serotonin. Exercise and other physical activities also produce endorphins, chemicals in the brain that act as natural painkillers, improve your mood and make you feel more relaxed. It can also improve the ability to sleep, which in turn reduces stress.

Another benefit of exercise is that it reactivates the prefrontal cortex, thereby mitigating your risk of succumbing to the hijacking amygdala. It helps to redirect attention towards values-aligned activities and away from perceived threats, reducing your anxiety reaction. Moving your body also reduces muscle tension and burns up those adrenaline stores.

Enjoy embracing the comprehensive exercise tips and strategies that were covered in your Mind Strength Toolkit (Take the first step; page 222). In summary, there are several ways to maximise the benefits of exercise and movement.

- Choose something enjoyable so you will do it repeatedly.
- Gradually increase the challenge so you work towards increasing your heart rate.

>>

- Consider planning your workouts with a friend or as part of an exercise group to include the added bonus of interpersonal connectedness.
- Where possible, exercise outdoors, further reducing stress and anxiety.
- Frequency is the most important contributor to success, so set small daily goals and aim for daily consistency rather than perfect workouts. For example, walk every day for 15–20 minutes, rather than waiting to do one big hit of exercise on the weekend.

Just connect

A foundation stone in the Mind Strength Wellbeing Pyramid is being socially connected. Connection with family, friends and the community is essential for your mental and physical wellbeing, and a protective factor against anxiety and depression. Authentic and values-aligned social connection provides happiness, security, support and a sense of purpose.

If anxiety is getting in the way of connecting with others, engaging in the strategies of the Mind Strength Method alongside working with a trained mental health practitioner can be very helpful. You can follow the steps mapped out in the Mind Strength Toolkit and build an action plan to gradually approach avoided situations while letting go of your safety behaviours. Worry might tell you to avoid social and interpersonal situations, so notice the worry story and be purposeful in approaching those situations instead.

Remember to take small steps out of your comfort zone. Once you do, the very act of connecting with others will be the confidence and mood booster you need to stretch that comfort zone further and keep up the momentum. This, in turn, will increase your sense of overall emotional wellbeing and create a positive wellbeing spiral. So ask yourself what social and interpersonal connections you would like to pursue but worry and anxiety have got in the way?

Write down the things that come to mind and see if you can treat these like behavioural experiments. Some examples

>>

of behavioural experiments that you can engage in to take steps out of your comfort zone and approach rather than avoid interpersonal connections include

- joining a group that is relevant to your interests
- enrolling in a class
- joining a sporting club or walking group
- joining an art or craft activity
- joining a social meet-up
- joining a book club
- volunteering for a charity or not-for-profit
- reaching out to the people around you.

Enjoy brainstorming the activities you have an interest in and set yourself small daily challenges. While immediate face-to-face communication and human touch are the best kinds of interpersonal connection, there are also many ways you can connect through digital technology.

If you want to get more out of your relationships, consider

- making a list of the people you want to contact regularly and adding a reminder in your calendar
- committing to a certain amount of time each day to spend with your family and the people you care about. This might include family time that is fixed each day, or time that you find around other commitments
- practising active listening and being conscious of not engaging in safety behaviours such as relying on your phone to distract you

- practising assertive communication and asking for
  help if you need it
- demonstrating your respect, support and appreciation
  for your friends and family by expressing your gratitude
- arranging a day out with friends you haven't seen
  for a while
- switching off the TV tonight and talking or playing
  a game with your partner or children
- having lunch with a work colleague
- visiting a friend or family member who needs support
  or company
- volunteering at a local school, hospital
  or community group.

If you are facing a particularly stressful or anxiety-provoking life experience, it can be helpful to enlist a support group of people beyond friends and family. A support group can provide

- deep connection with others who are going through similar
  experiences, reminding you that you are not alone
- inspiration and wisdom from others who are coping
- expert knowledge and practical suggestions from
  professionals who specialise in the specific area of concern.

Using the Mind Strength Toolkit to strengthen your relationship

You can now recognise that passivity, escape and avoidance, as well as finger-pointing, defensiveness, attacking, aggression and blame, are all unhelpful fight or flight reactions. Notice when these fight or flight actions are taking hold in your relationship. Ask yourself whether they serve any effective purpose. See if you and your partner can both build accountability to take steps out of fight or flight actions and realign with values-driven behaviours as a couple.

Be cautious of the negativity bias and all or nothing thinking, such as statements like, 'You never pay me attention.' Instead tip the focus towards problem-solving and action-planning, embracing a solution-oriented alternative, such as 'Could we spend an hour together soon?' Moving towards assertiveness using the strategies outlined on pages 249–50 will also be helpful.

If you feel that your relationship is stuck and you are having trouble expressing your feelings or getting your needs met, it can be helpful to engage a clinical psychologist or therapist specifically trained in relationship counselling. A therapist can also help you with tools and strategies to feel empowered to move out of relationships that make you feel unsafe, lower your self-esteem, trigger anxiety and are out of alignment with your values.

Mindfulness, meditation and relaxation

The next tier in the Mind Strength Wellbeing Pyramid relates to purposeful action to engage in mindfulness, meditation and relaxation. These help to quieten the sympathetic nervous system and realign with heart-driven engagement in the present moment.

MIND STRENGTH ACTION

Practise mindfulness

As you know from the Mind Strength Toolkit, mindfulness is your ability to step back from fight or flight driven thoughts, feelings and actions, and re-engage in the present moment with values-aligned clarity in any situation. It is intentionally observing and allowing your thoughts, emotions and sensations to just be, with purposeful, non-judgemental awareness.

By being fully aware of, and engaged in, what you are doing in the present moment, you are able to maintain some distance from your thoughts and not be reactive to them and your feelings. Rather than being distracted by worry about the future or rumination about the past, you can simply notice and acknowledge these experiences as thoughts and redirect your attention back to the present moment.

Mindfulness is core to the Mind Strength Method. It is recognising that the situation is not always in your control, but you can make purposeful choices in how you respond.

Try meditation

Meditation provides a training ground for learning to live mindfully. It provides a moment of stillness in the present moment amidst the uncertainty and complexity of daily life. Meditation is not about turning off thoughts and feelings. Rather, it helps you to get some distance from your thoughts and observe them and your feelings without judgement.

With consistent practice, meditation helps to strengthen the attention muscle, enabling you to become better at sustained focus in the present moment, rather than getting hooked in to the past or the future where rumination and worry lie. Meditation thus provides an antidote to the amygdala hijack and the anxiety triggered by focusing on worry and negative thoughts.

The purpose of meditation is not to get rid of anxiety. When you engage in meditation to get rid of anxiety, you end up putting yourself back in the boxing ring with anxiety, which keeps the fight or flight reaction active. Rather, meditation facilitates present moment awareness, with a reduction of anxiety as a byproduct of this skill.

There are many different types of meditation, including: mindfulness, spiritual, focused, movement, mantra and transcendental. The many different types of meditation all serve the powerful purpose of training your brain to experience sustained attention and the capacity to get some distance from the otherwise distracting nature of your thoughts. As the core ingredient across all meditation practices is facilitating mindful awareness, determine what feels right and comfortable for you. If one practice doesn't work for you, try another until you find one that does.

For example, transcendental meditation (TM) is a simple technique in which a personally assigned mantra such as a word, sound or short phrase is repeated in a specific way as a point of focus in your mind. The idea is that this technique allows you to settle inward to a deep state of relaxation and rest, with the goal of achieving inner peace without concentration or effort. Some people enjoy mantra meditation because they find it easier to focus on a word than on their breath. It is practised for 20 minutes twice each day while sitting comfortably with the eyes closed.

Mindfulness meditation originated from Buddhist teachings and is one of the most popular meditation techniques in the West. The main premise of mindfulness meditation is sustained attention in the present moment and allowing your thoughts to pass through your mind. It is observing and allowing the

>>

thoughts to just be in the present moment without judgement or getting involved in them. This practice combines concentration with awareness. For example, it might involve focusing on an object or on your breath while observing sensations, thoughts and feelings, and bringing your mind back to the present moment. There are plenty of apps and recordings on the internet that provide this type of meditation as an easy entry into meditation practice.

A basic mindful meditation practice is simply to focus on your breath. Paying attention to the breath and the sensations and experience of breathing helps you to maintain purposeful attention in the present moment. When the mind naturally wanders, as it will typically do, redirect your attention back to your breath.

Gentle, regular practice is helpful to experience the benefits of meditation over time. There is an abundance of scientific research to support the numerous and varied benefits of establishing a consistent meditation practice, with particular beneficial impacts on alleviating the experiences of anxiety and stress.

In fact, research demonstrates that not only does meditation assist in changing your mindset and perspective, but it also physically alters the brain through neuroplasticity. Brain imaging shows that activity in the grey matter, or the area of the brain responsible for emotional control, planning and problem-solving, increases with regular meditation practice. Similarly, the amygdala, which regulates how we feel stress, fear and anxiety, has been found to shrink through regular meditation practice.

Consistent meditation practice has also been found to alter the body's inherent stress response. Stress stimulates the sympathetic nervous system, triggering a surge of stress hormones into our bloodstream, such as adrenaline and cortisol. When the body and mind are relaxed through meditation practice or other relaxation techniques, the parasympathetic nervous system is activated, triggering the body's relaxation response, switching off the stress response and stress hormones of the sympathetic nervous system. In fact, people who meditate regularly develop the capacity to condition their body to relax on demand and switch off this stress reaction.

Whichever meditation technique you choose, the experience of mindfulness during meditation will make it easier for you to carry this skill through to your daily experiences. The more you can hone and develop your mindfulness practice through meditation, the more proficient you will be in catching yourself being distracted and bringing your focus back to the present moment.

It can be helpful to reflect on how your mind feels at the end of your meditation practice and make an intention to carry that experience into the remainder of your day. See if you can engage in the task straight after your meditation practice with the same level of purposeful awareness that you experienced throughout your meditation. Seek out opportunities throughout your day to reconnect with the mindfulness that you experienced in your meditation practice.

Make time to relax

The next component of the Mind Strength Wellbeing Pyramid is relaxation. Relaxation strategies refer to purposeful actions in your daily life that give you a sense of joy, tranquillity and fun, and serve to counteract your internal stress response. These are activities that facilitate focus on a task in the present moment. Different actions will trigger relaxation and calm for different people, depending on the activities they value; however, the common thread is that they facilitate mindful engagement in the present moment. Some common examples of relaxation activities of this nature include

- gardening
- bushwalking
- art and craft
- reading
- cooking
- sporting activities such as yoga, golf, surfing or sailing.

These activities will lift you from stress, anxiety and burnout, and will increase your ability to stay calm and collected under pressure. They will help to reinforce the strategies of the Mind Strength Method by facilitating present moment awareness. So have a think about some relaxation activities that you value and incorporate them into your action plan.

Gratitude and kindness

The next tier in the Mind Strength Wellbeing Pyramid is gratitude and kindness. As outlined in the Mind Strength Toolkit, there is compelling evidence that an attitude of gratitude and acts of kindness for yourself and others help to boost wellbeing and bolster you against mental health challenges.

Gratitude is the feeling of being thankful and appreciative. Kindness is when you act without expecting anything in return. Whether you're doing something kind for a stranger, a friend, a neighbour, a charity or yourself, kindness helps to provide a positive mood state for both you and others.

Gratitude and kindness have both been demonstrated to counteract the challenges of stress and anxiety. Expressions of gratitude and acts of kindness stimulate the production of serotonin, the feel-good neurochemical that serves to calm you down and lead to positive mood states. Kindness has been associated with the release of oxytocin, stimulating feelings of trust and connectedness. Engaging in acts of kindness and expressions of gratitude have also been found to produce an increase in endorphins and a reduction in the stress hormone, cortisol. By reducing the stress hormones and managing the autonomic nervous system functions, gratitude and kindness reduce symptoms of depression and anxiety.

Similarly, acts of kindness and gratitude have been associated with a boost in dopamine, and with feeling stronger, more positive and more energetic. Self-compassion is kindness turned inwards, which leads to a greater level of resilience, confidence and mental wellbeing.

Studies have also highlighted that regularly reflecting over a two-month period on the things you feel grateful for leads to a dramatic increase in optimism, which provides a strong tool in your toolkit to bolster you against anxiety. It rewires and trains the brain to be purposeful in seeing the good in things, and where you start to see things more positively, you start to experience greater happiness and wellbeing that endures over time.

When you practise gratitude and kindness, you are able to rebalance the hypervigilance to threat and the negativity bias that can take hold when the stress response has been triggered, and rebalance towards more positive and helpful evaluations of a situation. Studies have demonstrated that both serve to boost self-esteem in social situations, decrease social anxiety and significantly increase positive mood states.

Studies have also demonstrated that regular expressions of gratitude facilitate sleep onset and more peaceful sleep. Brain imaging has demonstrated that a regular practice of expressing gratitude through a journal or letter writing actually leads to changes in the brain through the process of neuroplasticity.

Given the abundance of evidence to support acts of kindness and expressions of gratitude to boost mental health and wellbeing, it is worthwhile including them in your weekly routine. These questions may help you identify opportunities to do this.

- Can you be purposeful in ending each day with things that you are grateful for?
- Can you try to do one small, kind thing each day for someone?

- Can you commit to noting down an act of kindness that you engaged in for yourself and others?
- Can you note down the impact these acts of gratitude and kindness have had on you?

By writing these down you build accountability and clarity around positive values-aligned actions. You also allow yourself to benefit from the feel-good neurochemicals that you get from reflecting on positive things. Typically, what we focus on grows, so when you are purposeful in your focus on your acts of kindness, the actions start to have a longer-lasting beneficial impact on your overall mood, along with reducing stress levels and an increase in positivity.

MIND STRENGTH ACTION

Keep a gratitude journal

Activities to express gratitude as a therapeutic tool might include keeping a gratitude journal where you reflect on and write down what you feel grateful for, a regular gratitude meditation, listing three things you feel grateful for every night, or commencing your day reflecting on something you feel grateful for. Active daily practice is recommended to cement the positive impacts on mental health and wellbeing.

Gratitude journalling specifically can help to lower your stress levels and help you feel calmer especially at night. Journalling can also give you a new perspective on the things that are important to you and what you appreciate. It helps to

>>

build self-awareness and can serve as a powerful reminder to realign with values-driven goals and actions. On days when you feel more anxious or down, you can read through your gratitude journal to readjust and rebalance. A gratitude journal can also help to make you more mindful, balanced and grounded in the present. It encourages you to notice the small, good things that are happening, and acts as a beacon to positive experiences and accomplishments.

The following tips can be useful for maintaining a gratitude journal:

- Although any time of the day to write in your journal is beneficial, it can be helpful to build it into your daily routine.

- Consider setting a daily reminder or schedule it in your calendar.

- Consider writing in your gratitude journal every night for 15 minutes before going to bed. Doing your gratitude reflections at night can be beneficial as it incorporates things from your day and helps you to stimulate those positive neurochemicals before going to sleep. Keeping your gratitude journal on your bedside table can make it easier to stick with this as a daily routine.

- If you have more time, don't feel like you need to rush through the process – savouring expressions of gratitude can be a great exercise.

The power of association can work to make even simply looking at your journal something that serves to reduce stress and anxiety, and boost your overall sense of wellbeing. Write as many things as you want in your gratitude journal; about five things that you are grateful for each day is a good number to aim for, but allow for flexibility that sometimes there will be more and sometimes less. The items on your list can be simple or complex – it's all good! Keep the practice a regular part of your day for at least three weeks, to give yourself a good chance of establishing and consolidating a new habit in order to experience the benefits.

Be conscious of not just going through the motions of expressions of gratitude. Engaging mindfully in the process of writing down what you feel grateful for will lead to a more potent outcome. It can also help you to notice when worry thoughts are leading you astray and bring you back to the present moment. Write down what you are grateful for and then consider elaborating on why you are grateful, to further consolidate the experience of gratitude. This reflection can also clarify the things that are truly important for you in life and keep you aligned with Step 2 of the Mind Strength Method – your values.

The following is a list of gratitude prompts to get your gratitude creativity flowing.

- People in your life you feel grateful for and the reasons why
- Skills and abilities you are grateful for

>>

>> *Keep a gratitude journal – continued*

- A challenge or opportunity for learning and growth
- Positive changes you are grateful for
- Activities and hobbies
- Things you like about your city, suburb or town
- The best parts of your day
- Qualities in the people who are challenging in your life
- Tangible items you are grateful for
- Music and other forms of entertainment
- People who have helped you in the past
- Food or drinks
- Things in nature and the environment
- Things that you have learned
- Memories
- Experiences at work
- Sensory experiences

Values and purpose

At the pinnacle of the Mind Strength Wellbeing Pyramid is alignment with your professional and personal purpose and values. Clarity on your values, and proactive engagement in a values-driven direction with goal and action alignment, are the essence of empowerment. They are core to the Mind Strength Method and essential to curbing anxiety, conquering worry and building resilience.

Chapter 25

Enjoy mind strength

You are now equipped with a
Mind Strength Toolkit for life

Now that you are skilled in the Mind Strength Method, you are equipped with a powerful, practical toolkit for life. The strategies you have learned are ones that you can apply personally, professionally and academically.

I encourage you to maintain self-awareness around your fight or flight driven thoughts, feelings and actions. Go back through the chapters of this book and use it as a resource for life. Notice, pivot and realign with the wisdom provided by clarity on your values, purpose, goals and actions. Move from worry and concern around the things that are out of your control to problem-solving and action-planning around the things that are in your control. Be super proud of yourself for the efforts that you take to stand up to worry, to approach rather than avoid and to allow yourself to build resilience.

Remember that to be human is to feel emotions, to experience vulnerability and to be imperfect. The situation is not always in your control but the Mind Strength Method is your power to create space between the situation and how you choose to respond to it. Worry and your amygdala will want you to be hijacked by fear, anxiety, anger and agitation. As a cave-person, you would have been a protector wanting to keep your tribe safe from predators and threats. Now, in our highly complex, uncertain world, you are equipped with a Mind Strength Toolkit that is more aligned with our times. Our world requires you to sit with uncertainty. You now know how to stand up to worry, how to quieten that feisty amygdala, and how to stretch your comfort zone to embrace the life that you want, not the life that worry is telling you to live.

You have many wonderful qualities, values and strengths. These are wrapped up in your fabulous, caring heart. This is where your power lies; your heart serves you well. It will pull you in a values-aligned direction. Take your focus there now.

- What is it telling you?
- What places does it want you to go?
- What passions does it want you to embrace?
- What opportunities does it want you to serve?
- What problems does it want you to solve?

Congratulations on embracing the Mind Strength Method. Enjoy this process and enjoy using the toolkit as you move from anxiety, stress, worry and fear to empowered, confident and resilient action. It's my life's mission to help people in this quest to move from anxiety to action and to build mind strength. It has been an honour and a pleasure, and I wish you all the best on your journey through life.

Acknowledgements

The Mind Strength Method has been a labour of love and I am deeply grateful to the many people who have helped in its delivery.

My heartfelt thanks goes to Murdoch Books and Allen & Unwin. Living life with mind strength is about clarity on, and alignment with, values-driven actions and from the moment I met Lou Johnson and Jane Morrow I knew that these exceptional professionals were deeply values-aligned. Thanks to you both for your expertise and for being the perfect people to help me in my mission to share a positive and empowering narrative on anxiety to help people on scale. This alignment has permeated through the entire Murdoch team and I am so grateful to you all – Justin, Ariane, Astred, Susanne, Viv, Julie, Britta, Sarah, Jemma and everyone else who has contributed – thank you for your exceptional skills, positivity and heartfelt commitment to helping people with anxiety.

I am beyond grateful to my teams at The Anxiety Clinic, Dr Jodie and Mind Strength for your passionate and positive commitment to helping me every step of the way. To my valued clients – the parents, kids, teens, couples, families and adults seeking our help at The Anxiety Clinic and to the leaders, organisations and schools who engage our Mind Strength Peak Performance and Resilience programs and keynotes – my deepest gratitude for the insights you have provided in the growth and development of the Mind Strength Method and for your continued inspiration. Seeing the transformation in each of you is my energy, my motivation and my joy.

To Viktor Frankl and the giants of CBT, ACT, Compassion Focused Therapy, mindfulness and other evidence-based modalities, thank you for being pivotal in my professional development and for being core to the strategies contained in this book. To Brené Brown and other strong leaders in the world of resilience, high performance, mental health and wellbeing, thank you for your incredible inspiration.

To my beautiful friends, thank you for being an ever-flowing source of care and insights.

Thank you to you, the reader, for sharing your time with me through the pages of this book. I look forward to staying connected with each of you as part of the Dr Jodie and Mind Strength Facebook and other online and in person communities. Please share this book with your family and friends; together we can create a Mind Strength Movement to help people worldwide curb anxiety, conquer worry and build resilience.

And finally, thank you to my truly amazing family; my love for you is boundless and I wake each morning with a heart filled with gratitude. Your love, laughs, kindness and resilience are my inspiration. May you always be a rock for each other and be motivated by the goodness in each of you. I hope that the ideas contained within *The Mind Strength Method* continue to inspire you just as you inspire me daily.

REFERENCES

To view a complete list of references used for this book, go to drjodie.com.au or visit the Murdoch Books website (murdochbooks. com.au) and search for *The Mind Strength Method*.

Index